CONTENTS

Opposite: Two-sided sheet of studies: Head of an old man, and studies of machinery (verso, ill. opposite), Studies for the Christ Child with a lamb (recto, ill. op. 8), c. 1503-6. This sheet is characteristic of Leonardo's working method, mixing quick sketches, technical drawing and commentary (this side), with swift, but carefully considered compositional ideas (other side)

INTRODUCTION

CHARLES ROBERTSON

Is there any artist more famous than Leonardo da Vinci? The texts selected here, either written in Leonardo da Vinci's lifetime or in the half century after his death, show how a powerful persona or myth was created. As always in history, it is hard to separate the facts from the imaginative evocation of second and third hand accounts. Giorgio Vasari's *Life of Leonardo da Vinci, Painter and Sculptor of Florence* from his *Lives of the Most Excellent Painters, Sculptors and Architects*, by far our most important source of information on Leonardo's life, is a case in point: as a printed book aimed at the new audience printing had created, it had to be entertaining as well as informative.

This version of the *Life* is from Vasari's second edition, published in Florence in 1568. The augmented version of his first edition of 1550 continues to provide

Opposite, other side of the sheet ill. p. 7: here Leonardo explores different poses for the Christ Child with a lamb, probably a study for the Virgin and Child with St John, lost but known through copies

many frames of reference for discussion of Leonardo. It can be read here alongside a selection of other texts. Two are overtly biographical: the earlier life or eulogy by Paolo Giovio, connected to but not actually included with Giovio's *Lives of Famous Men*, first published in 1549; and the selection of fragmentary anecdotes about artists collected in Florence around 1530 by an unidentified writer known as the Anonimo Gaddiano. (He has also been called the Anonimo Fiorentino, from his town of origin; 'Gaddiano' refers to an early owner of the manuscript, as does another alternative name, the Anonimo Magliabecchiano. Various identities have been suggested, but one thing is certain: that the writer knew Vasari.) Vasari, the Anonimo and Giovio were also aware of the basic information about Leonardo's works and their location first recorded around 1522 in a book of notes about artists that belonged to the Florentine merchant Antonio Billi and was probably written by him.

Leonardo also made more literary guest appearances in printed books by two Milanese writers. A minor humanist and collector, Sabba da Castiglione, gave his assessment in his *Ricordi ovvero ammaestramenti,* a kind of commonplace book published in 1554. In the same year Matteo Bandello, probably writing from memory, gave a description of Leonardo's working methods in one of his so-called novels, a collection of imaginative stories and anecdotes of contemporary life. Vasari was able to draw on these sources; what he would not have known are the letters by Leonardo or concerning him that are also included here, but these primary sources make it clear that many themes favoured by Vasari and other secondary sources were indeed grounded in fact.

The facts of Leonardo's life are fairly well established. He was born, illegitimately, in rural Tuscany in 1452, and trained as a youth in Florence with the sculptor-painter Andrea Verrocchio (other members of the studio included Perugino). In 1476 he was acquitted of sodomy, notoriously rife in Florence. He went to Milan in 1482, where he remained for 17 years, establishing himself as a court artist, and also musician and engineer. The *Last Supper* (ill. pp. 58-60) dates from this period, but much of Leonardo's time was taken up with a project for a monumental bronze horse and rider, which was never completed. In 1500, following the French invasion, he transferred to Florence and worked for the Republic there, and for other patrons such as the great soldier Cesare Borgia. From 1506 to 1513 Leonardo was back in Milan (working particularly on anatomy for a projected book of engravings) and from 1513 to 1516 he was in Rome. Works such as the *Virgin and Child with St Anne* (ill. p. 119) date from this later period. In 1516 he moved to France as court artist to the king, Francis I, and he died there in 1519.

Vasari was not, however, simply interested in writing the facts of the lives of his artists. Every *Life* is designed to be exemplary: that is, to demonstrate a particular aspect of artistic life and endeavour. This is particularly true for Vasari's key artists: Leonardo, Raphael and Michelangelo, the principal figures of his climactic third period, which coincides with the later critical notion of the 'High Renaissance'. Here Raphael was the charming, brilliant genius, and Michelangelo the realization of perfection in modern art. Leonardo's status is not so straightforward, not least because he was substantially older than the other two, with much of his work completed before 1500. But his position in Vasari's scheme is crucial. It is Leonardo's *Life* that starts Part 3, and it comes immediately after the preface, in which Vasari has made his case for the massive achievement of modern art, its naturalism contrasted with the rigid, formulaic work of the 15th-century painters:

> Their error was afterwards clearly proved by the works of Leonardo da Vinci, who, giving a beginning to that third manner which we propose to call the modern—besides the force and boldness of his drawing, and the extreme subtlety wherewith he counterfeited all the minutiæ of nature exactly as they are—with good rule, better order, right proportion, perfect drawing, and divine grace, abounding in resources and having a most

> profound knowledge of art, may be truly said to have endowed his figures with motion and breath . . .

So keen is Vasari to place Leonardo as a founder of modern art, that he omits Ariosto's prominent namecheck in Canto 33 of *Orlando Furioso*, published in 1532. This was a notable validation of the artist's standing, in which Ariosto, the leading poet of the age, drew a flattering parallel between modern painters, with Leonardo first in the list, and the great artists of antiquity. Vasari was aware of the passage, and indeed alludes to it in his *Life* of Mantegna. That he ignores it in the *Life* of Leonardo begs the question: does Vasari's scheme of modern painting stand up? Surprisingly, perhaps in view of its longevity as an idea — for centuries Leonardo, Raphael and Michelangelo were held up as the prime exemplars of the greatest style — the answer is no. In fact the two painters mentioned by Ariosto in the same line, Mantegna and Bellini, have as good a claim to be the founders of modern art. Mantegna set a neoclassical course which remained relevant until the Carracci and Poussin, while Bellini's handling of oil paint bridges the transition from

Overleaf: View of Montelupo Castle and the valley of the Arno, 5 August 1473. Leonardo's oldest surviving drawing, this is also one of the first pure landscapes in Western art. Leonardo continued to be fascinated by high places throughout his life

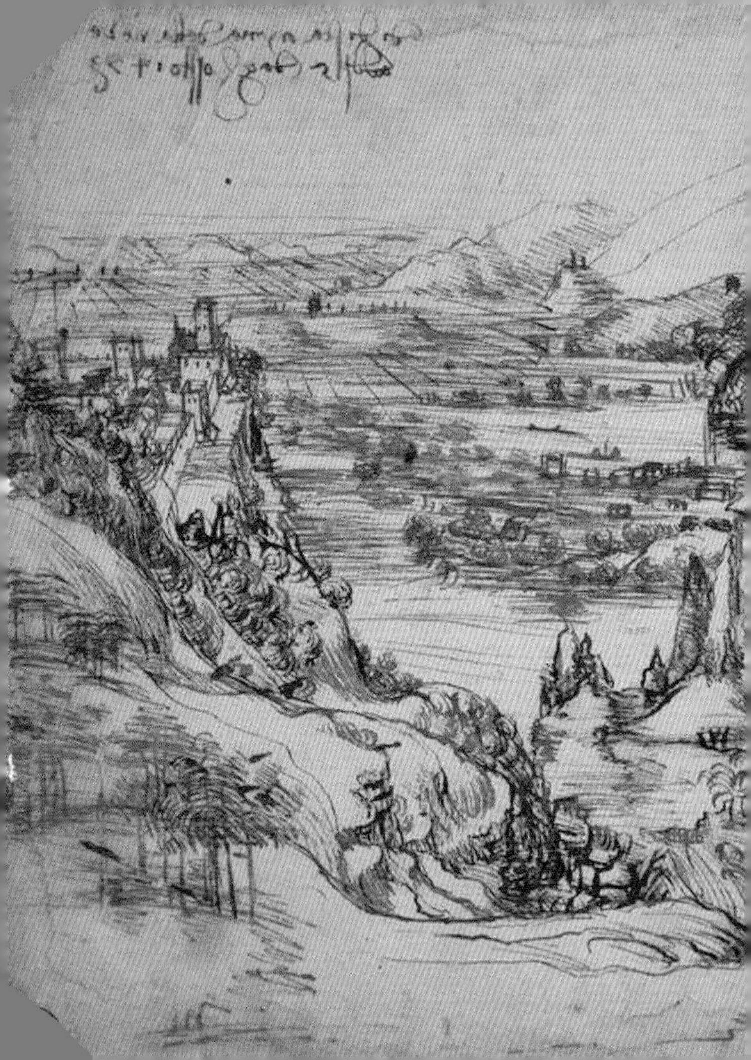

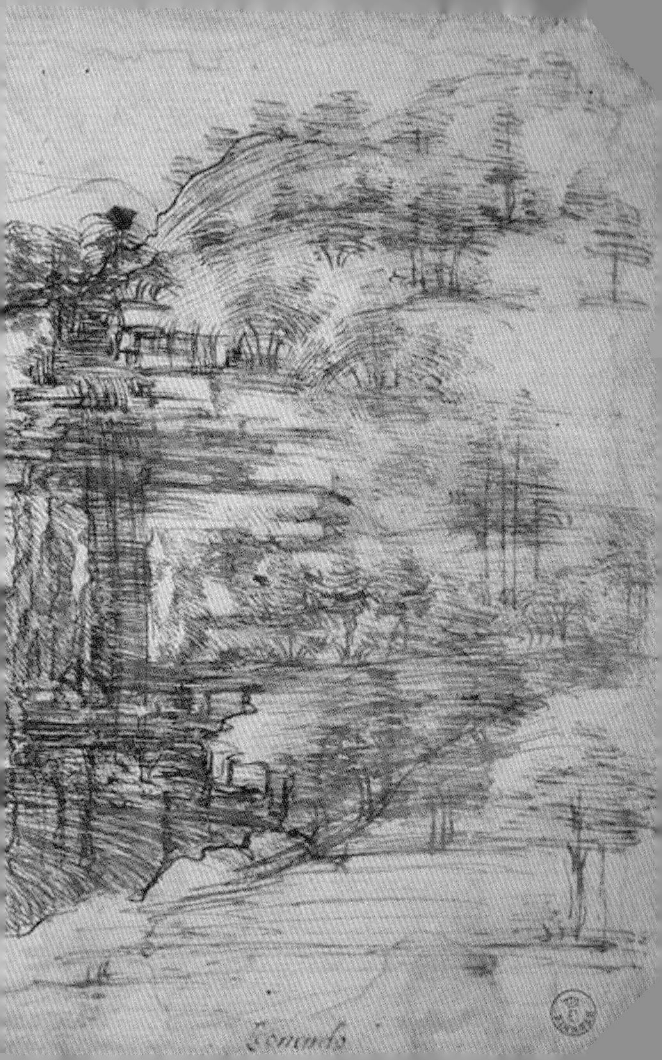

hard-edged to soft painting. Nor did Leonardo shift the paradigm for painting in the way that Donato Bramante did for architecture. Moreover his achievement as an artist could not equal that of Raphael or Michelangelo simply because the number of substantial works he managed to complete was significantly less.

Vasari allowed his heroizing tendency to affect the details of the biography too. An example is his discussion of Leonardo's early training with Verrocchio. This of course is an essential element from the biographical point of view, but rather than taking the opportunity to explain Leonardo's education, Vasari draws a contrast between the youthful genius and plodding older painter. Leonardo paints the head of an angel in his master's *Baptism*, now in the Uffizi (ill. p. 45), so brilliantly that according to Vasari Verrocchio gave up painting altogether. It is an object lesson in the superiority of the third period over the second; indeed it might be seen as the demarcation. That in fact Leonardo's practice drew deeply on contemporary practice, deriving much from artists around him such as Filippo Lippi, could not be acknowledged in such a discussion. (The *Annunciation*, ill. pp. 18-19, which Vasari does not mention and may not have known, shows how mainstream Leonardo in fact was at this stage.)

Nonetheless, when we come to the *Life* itself, we are

in for something of a surprise, since it is somewhat hard to match the paragon amongst painters suggested in the preface. Leonardo emerges as an extraordinary character, but one whose achievement is significantly compromised by failure to complete work, or indeed by the technical failure of the work itself, as in the case of the *Battle of Anghiari* (ill. p. 81), where the use of oil paint directly on the walls was almost immediately disastrous. Why does Vasari knock down his ideal in this apparently illogical way? In part, it's a function of the critical structure of the book. It is only natural that there might be a difference between the theoretical positions of the prefaces and the biographical impetus of an individual life. Indeed, to be valid the individual *Lives* need to convey the humanity of the subject, and this could well include eccentricity. To find inconsistency in this dual system misses the point. The *Lives* are a complex work and each element is required to stand on its own.

It is easier to understand Vasari's strategy if we remember that he was not writing in a vacuum. He enjoyed the support and interest of many distinguished intellectuals, whose authority was great because they were of higher social status than him. Indeed one of these other writers was Paolo Giovio, who had already embarked on a series of lives of famous men and women and who was, according to Vasari's own account, the man who encouraged

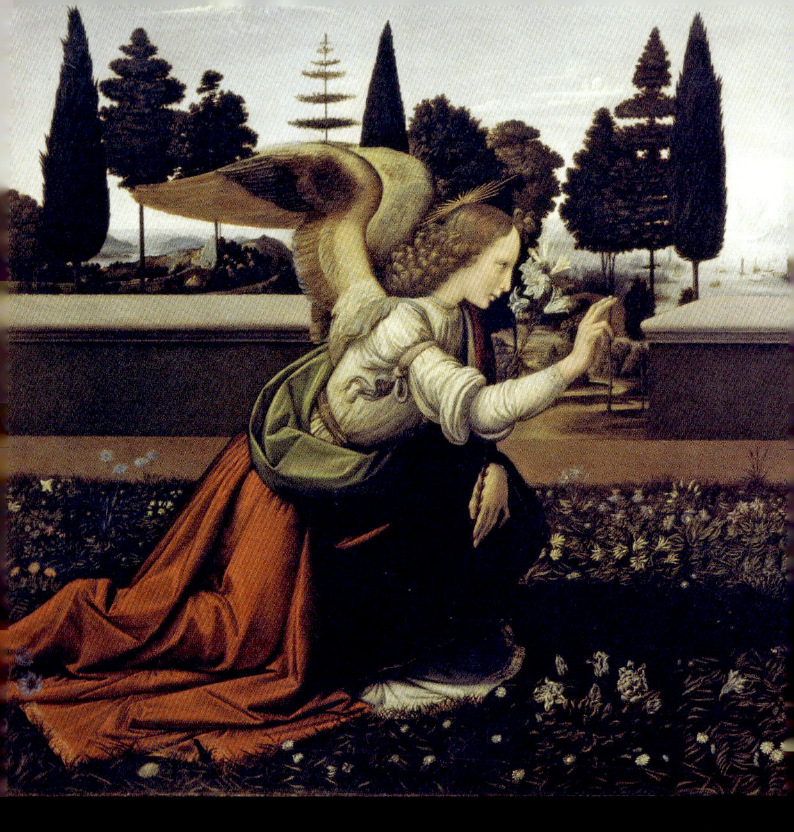

The Annunciation, 1472-76. Leonarrdo's earliest surviving painting, possibly in collaboration with Andrea Verrocchio

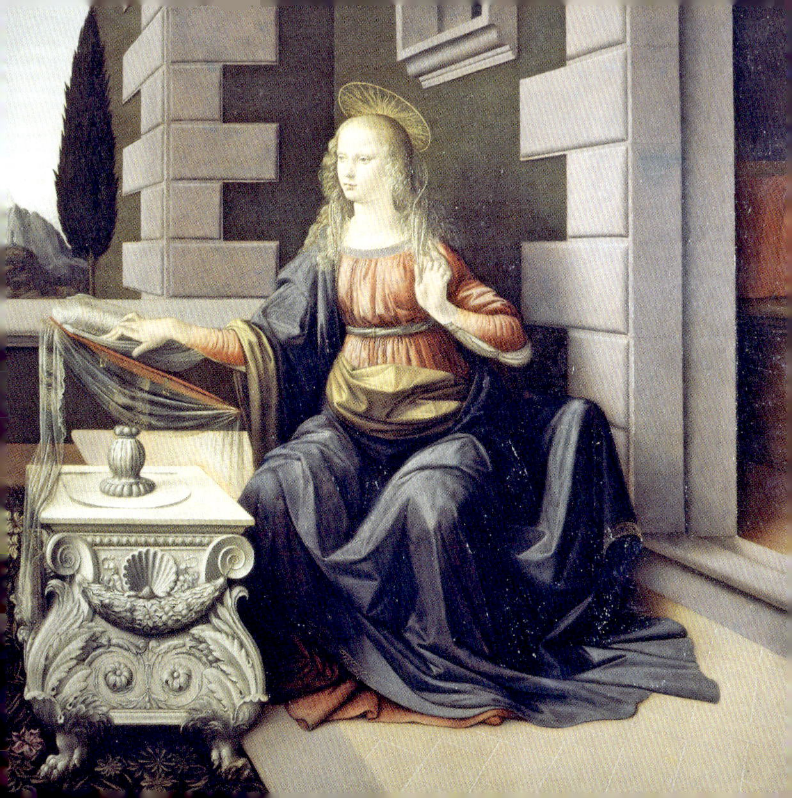

him to write the *Lives* in the first place. Even here, Vasari may be embroidering to give his project more credibility, as he was in fact already collecting material before he met Giovio in Rome in the late 1540s. Ironically this search for evidence is far more reminiscent of a modern historian, and now seems a more respectable endeavour than Giovio's collection of exemplary lives.

Yet we should always be careful to recognise that Vasari was writing history on his own terms, and in terms of the expectations of his audience and certainly not history of art in our terms. What that meant was drawing on all the various ancient models, particularly Pliny the Elder's *Natural History*, with the concentration on material, anecdote and rhetorical traditions of praise and blame. In this way the *Life* of Leonardo is a composite of factual description and rhetorical creation. Somewhat short on detailed information, Vasari makes up for it with a vivid evocation of the extraordinary and delightful character of Leonardo and his work. His Leonardo is a person of remarkable beauty who lives like a nobleman, dressed in fine clothes, with servants and horses, although it is never clear how this fine life was paid for. Vasari's efforts to describe the man are almost as if he is hoping this impression might excuse the indeterminate nature of the

Opposite: Masquerader on horseback, 1517-18

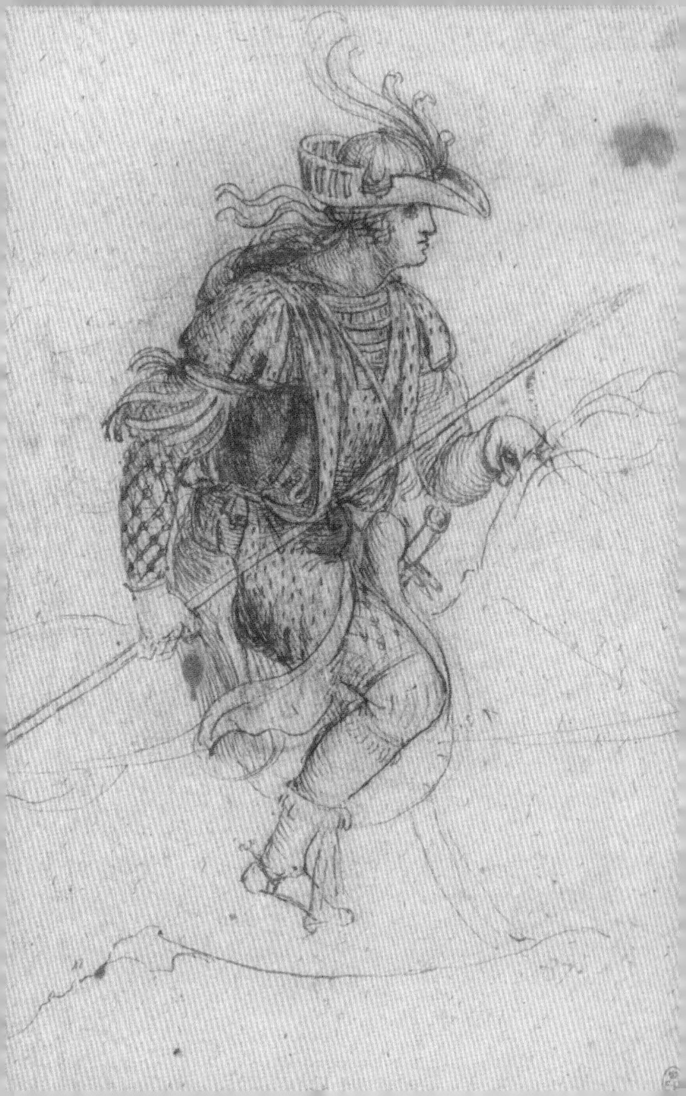

achievement. Perhaps this reflects the reality. Leonardo was extraordinarily persuasive and could stimulate the patrons to impossible undertakings. This aspect of his personality is borne out by the 1482 draft of a letter, included here, setting out what he can do for the Duke of Milan as a military engineer. Vasari does not altogether ignore the time-wasting: in his account of Leonardo's conduct in Rome, around 1514, we see him failing to complete substantial works but indulging instead in elaborate games to delight a court, including spectacular inflatable animals. Again, this disinclination to productive work in favour of intellectual pursuits is confirmed by a number of the letters included here, while the related inclination to maintain an almost noble household and appreciate the finer things of life is confirmed by Leonardo himself in the *Paragone*: in those theoretical notes on art, which included an extended comparison between painting and sculpture, the painter is portrayed wearing beautiful clothes, in contrast to the coarse dirty manual work of the sculptor.

At another level, Vasari is also constructing a good story to entertain the reader, and his anecdotes reflect this impulse too. A good example is the story of the rough circular piece of wood, cut from a fig tree, which one of Leonardo's father's peasants desired to have painted. Leonardo decided to create an extraordinarily horrifying head of Medusa, composed of multiple elements derived from the most copious exploration of nature. When completed, he cleverly manipulated its viewing by placing it in a darkened room with ingenious lighting effects. Leonardo's father sold the work at profit and eventually it was acquired by the Duke of Milan (it has since been lost). The naive peasant received instead a crude image of a heart pierced by an arrow and was entirely happy. Beyond the ironic contrast of the sophisticated and popular imagery, this story shows an unusual interest in reception and is also a device to point to the development of Leonardo's career in Milan.

Although Vasari's *Life* is billed as that of Leonardo the painter and sculptor, one aspect that is perhaps inevitably downplayed is Leonardo's work in sculpture Partly this was because here Leonardo's debt to Verrocchio, another practicioner of both arts, was most obvious. As we saw earlier, the master was cast as fall-guy to the young genius, and so his crucial contribution to this side of his pupil's formation could not be acknowledged. The great equestrian monument in Milan to Duke Francesco Sforza, the father of Leonardo's patron Lodovico il Moro, is the main sculpture with which Leonardo was associated and one which is mentioned by most early sources. The failure to achieve the giant project is noted as an inevitability because of its intended scale, and as yet another proof of Leonardo's impractical genius. In the Anonimo Gaddiano's account the sculpture was a pretext for the young Michelangelo to criticise the older master, who was a hated rival. Vasari uses a rhetorical smokescreen to mitigate this failure, repeatedly embroidering the theme of horses throughout the text. Leonardo confirms his own almost noble status by keeping horses himself; he proves his brilliance to the Duke of Milan by creating a wonderful silver lyre in the form of a horse's head; he mastered equine anatomy in extraordinary drawings and near the end of his career brilliantly represents horses in his abortive mural of the *Battle of Anghiari* for the council chamber of the Florentine Republic, the wonders of which Vasari details. Finally in order to prove Leonardo's godlike status Vasari says that in addition to his great beauty he had superhuman strength and could bend horseshoes. With such deft accretion, Vasari rendered the somewhat problematic reality powerful and attractive.

These complexities in Vasari's text point to the fact that Leonardo da Vinci was at the cusp was of the information revolution wrought through the development of printing, both texts and images. He was the dedicatee of the first printed vernacular text on art, *Prospectivo*

Opposite: Studies of horses' legs, c. 1490; preparation for the Sforza monument

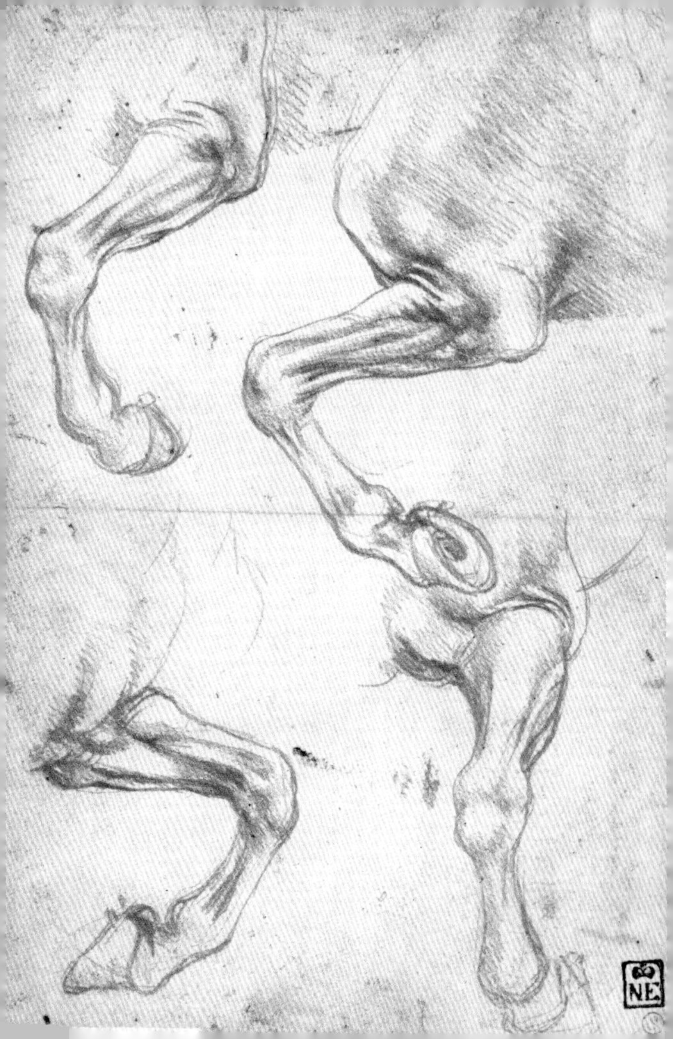

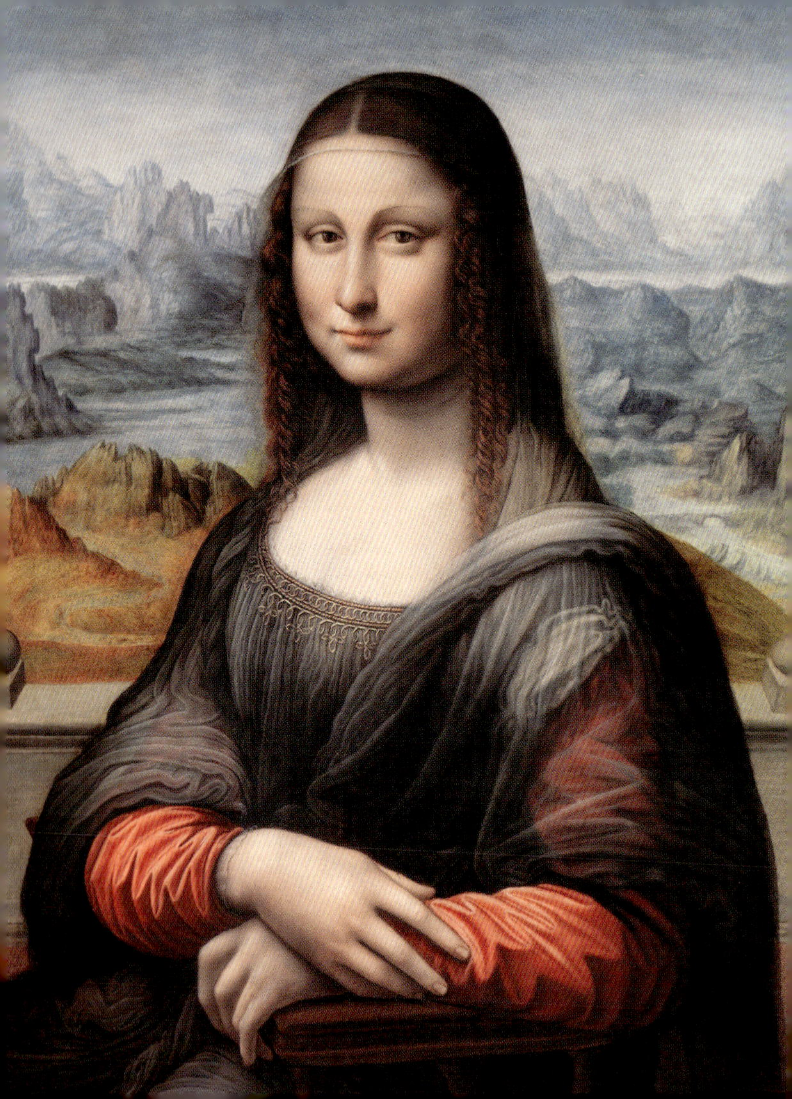

melanese depictore Antiquarie prospetiche romane, a poem devoted to antiquities of Rome by one of his Milanese associates. After his death he is mentioned in a number of printed texts, among them the *Novelle* of Matteo Bandello, an excerpt of which is included here, and the passage in Ariosto alluded to above.

Vasari was fully aware of the possibilities and requirements of the new medium and its public. A striking example is the fulsome passage of word-painting in which he describes the *Mona Lisa*. Clearly he felt the painting was famous enough that his audience would expect a full description of what they could never see for themselves. But his description reveals that Vasari had not seen it either. He praises Leonardo's handling of the eyebrows and the eyelashes, which are non-existent in the painting in Paris. Instead, Vasari must have been working from a copy made by assistants under Leonardo's supervision, and now in Madrid. It's a useful reminder that compared to us, Vasari knew few pictures. His travels and his interest would have allowed him to see more than his potential readers, but still relatively little. Nor, despite the increasing popularity of prints, could readers rely on engravings of Leonardo's work as they might to

Opposite: Unknown assistant of Leonardo, Mona Lisa, c. 1503-19. This version in the Prado, Madrid, is probably by Salai or Francesco Melzi

some extent for Raphael and Michelangelo. An exception Vasari highlights is the fine sequence of engravings of the obsessive Knot Patterns, though Vasari characterizes these as a waste of time, however impressive (see ill. p. 161). Even the engravings after the *Last Supper* were markedly coarse, and astonishingly it was not until the beginning of the 19th century that a truly authoritative engraved version was made by the German-Neapolitan printmaker Raffaello Sanzio Morghen.

Thus it is perhaps not surprising that Vasari should have considered the Prado *Mona Lisa* an autograph painting — he had little to compare it to. In fact, few of the paintings we now think of as part of the Leonardo canon were accessible. But we can also wonder if, in the case of the *Mona Lisa*, Vasari would have cared overmuch. Duplication of images was very much standard practice; any workshop, Leonardo's included, reused designs to produce paintings with varying degrees of personal involvement by the master. It was the creation of the initial design that was the master's most important contribution; and in the case of Leonardo, a reluctant painter it seems at the best of times, this usual pattern was reinforced by his physical inability to paint in later years, as recorded by de Beatis and Novellara.

Nevertheless the particular atmosphere of Leonardo's paintings was famous, and Vasari's achievement in evoking it in his descriptions is truly remarkable. Possibly it is a reflection of the importance of Leonardo's example to his own practice as a painter of light and shade:

> It is an extraordinary thing how that genius, in his desire to give the highest relief to the works that he made, went so far with dark shadows, in order to find the darkest possible grounds, that he sought for blacks which might make deeper shadows and be darker than other blacks, that by their means he might make his lights the brighter; and in the end this method turned out so dark, that, no light remaining there, his pictures had rather the character of things made to represent an effect of night, than the clear quality of daylight.

More accessible and numerous than the paintings, and arguably more important in understanding Leonardo's contribution to art, were his drawings, and indeed some of Vasari's readers might have remembered the public exhibition of the St Anne cartoon. Vasari was a pioneer in the collection of drawings and in particular had some beautiful drapery studies by Leonardo. He writes interestingly about different kinds of drawing Leonardo did. These included a highly finished drawing of Neptune and a cartoon for a tapestry to cover a door made for the King of Portugal, representing Adam and

Eve. This was notable for the beautiful representation of trees. He vividly described this which recalls one on the most important recoveries of recent times, the astounding foliage in the wreaths surrounding the coats of arms in the lunettes about the *Last Supper*. Vasari is also informative about a kind of imaginative drawing Leonardo did where he would look intently at his subject and then return home to draw from memory — a point that underlines the fact that very often, Renaissance drawing was imaginative rather than explicitly life drawing.

One remarkable aspect of the *Life* is a passage on meaning describing that publicly exhibited cartoon, now lost:

> not without a smile from St Anne, who, overflowing with joy, was beholding her earthly progeny become divine – ideas truly worthy of the brain and genius of Leonardo.

Nor was Vasari alone in being interested in meaning, as in 1501 Fra Pietro da Novellara had written to Isabella d'Este, the Marchioness of Mantua, a passionate patron of contemporary art, about another cartoon which was

Opposite: Studies of the Virgin adoring the Christ Child, c. 1480-85. In this sheet of sketches Leonardo imagines several widely differing approaches to the meaning of the Virgin's relationship with her Son, in some cases including the infant St John

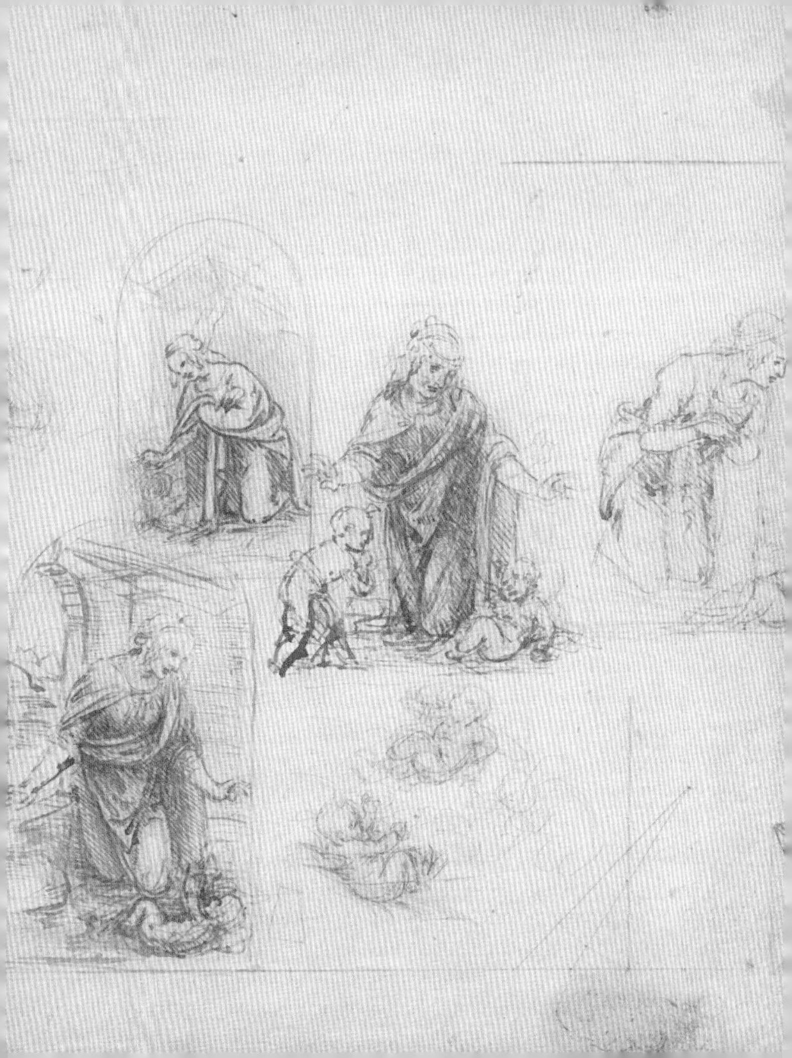

eventually realized in the painting of the *Virgin and St Anne*, now in the Louvre (ill. p. 119):

> The mother half rising from the lap of St Anne is catching the child to draw it away from the lamb, that sacrificial animal which signifies the Passion. St Anne, just rising from her seat, as if she would wish to hinder her daughter from parting the Child from the lamb; which perhaps signifies the Church that would not wish the Passion of Christ to be hindered.

Such concern with issue of meaning is unusual in writing about art at the period. This is not to say that meaning was not key, but it was often simply assumed. Vasari's explicit emphasis probably reflects Leonardo's own preoccupation, and it was clearly part of the reaction that his work elicited.

Vasari called Leonardo the painter and sculptor of Florence and indeed that was true of his birth and upbringing. However it is also misleading, since a very large proportion of his career was spent in Milan: seventeen years from 1483 to 1500, and some more in the new century. Unfortunately Vasari's localism has often resulted in a Florentine bias in later criticism. He had little knowledge or understanding of Leonardo's Milanese experience, although a brief visit to Milan before revising the second edition led him to augment this section, particularly in relation to the *Last Supper*. By contrast with his Florentine period, it also possible to see Leonardo as quite an effective court artist despite the failure of the Sforza monument, for, as well executing the *Last Supper,* he seems to have been responsible for overseeing decorations in the Castle, notably the Sala delle Asse. The account of his burial in France in 1519, describing him as the 'Ex-director of painting for the Duke of Milan', implies a regular, if humdrum career. Added to his court responsibilities, he had significant employment beyond, producing the two versions of the *Madonna of the Rocks* (ill. p. 111). He also had important interactions with local artists in Milan; Vasari mentions his pupils, and it is indeed a significant fact that Leonardo as much as any Renaissance artist created a group of followers or imitators.

Some were close collaborators, as it seems that many of his works were joint productions, an important point made by Antonio de Beatis in the letter describing Leonardo in France at the end of his life, when he was no longer painting but overseeing an assistant. This final phase marked the culmination of success as a court artist with a pension from the king, Francis I. In a crowning myth, the painter and celebrator of painters Vasari has his fellow artist die in the arms of the great monarch.

Leonardo da Vinci was and is very famous and because

of this, caution is required, as each period has created its own version of the artist. In our own time these range from Sigmund Freud's psychoanalytical approach to the prevalent notion of Leonardo as a kind of proto-scientist, problematic given that the notion of science is quite a modern one. Such approaches should not be discounted since, even if anachronistic, they bear testimony to the continuing power of the artist. However the very plethora of new interpretations gives a particular value to the early sources by Vasari and his contemporaries which can take the reader close to Leonardo in a particularly engaging way.

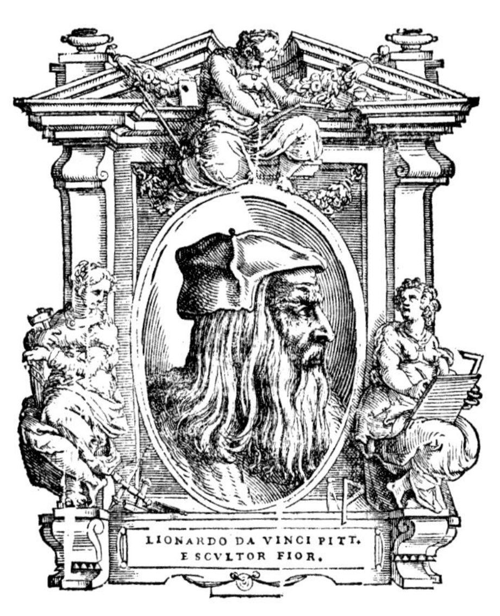

The Life of Leonardo da Vinci
Painter and Sculptor of Florence

GIORGIO VASARI

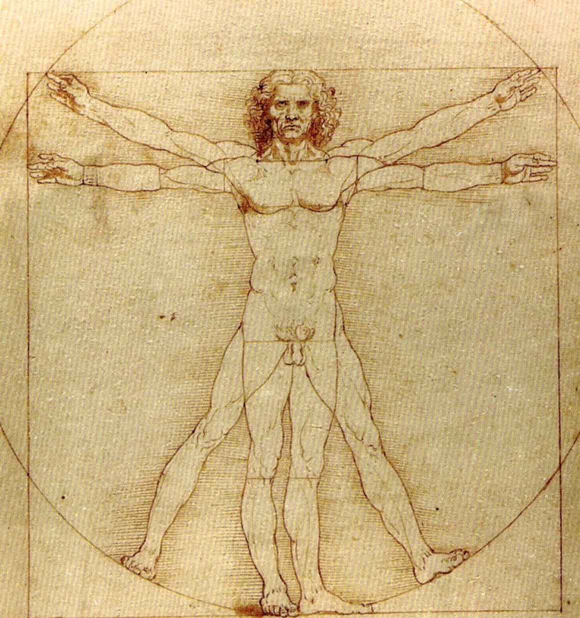

The greatest gifts are often seen, in the course of nature, rained by celestial influences on human creatures; and sometimes, in supernatural fashion, beauty, grace, and talent are united beyond measure in one single person, in a manner that to whatever such an one turns his attention, his every action is so divine, that, surpassing all other men, it makes itself clearly known as a thing bestowed by God (as it is), and not acquired by human art. This was seen by all mankind in Leonardo da Vinci, in whom, besides a beauty of body never sufficiently extolled, there was an infinite grace in all his actions; and so great was his genius, and such its growth, that to whatever difficulties he turned his mind, he solved them with ease. In him was great bodily strength, joined to dexterity, with a spirit and courage ever royal and magnanimous; and the fame of his name so increased, that not only in his lifetime was he held in esteem, but his reputation became even greater among posterity after his death.

Truly marvellous and celestial was Leonardo, the son of Ser Piero da Vinci; and in learning and in the rudiments of letters he would have achieved great proficiency, if he had not been so variable and

Opposite: 'Vitruvian Man', c. 1490. This image of the proportions of the human body according to the architect Vitruvius is sometimes thought to be a self-portrait

unstable, for he set himself to learn many things, and then, after having begun them, abandoned them. Thus, in arithmetic, during the few months that he studied it, he made so much progress, that, by continually suggesting doubts and difficulties to the master who was teaching him, he would very often bewilder him. He gave some little attention to music, and quickly resolved to learn to play the lyre, as one who had by nature a spirit most lofty and full of refinement: wherefore he sang divinely to that instrument, improvising upon it. Nevertheless, although he occupied himself with such a variety of things, he never ceased drawing and working in relief, pursuits which suited his fancy more than any other. Ser Piero, having observed this, and having considered the loftiness of his intellect, one day took some of his drawings and carried them to Andrea del Verrocchio, who was his particular friend, and asked him directly to say whether Leonardo, by devoting himself to drawing, would achieve any proficiency. Andrea was astonished to see the extraordinary beginnings of Leonardo, and urged Ser Piero that he should make him study it; wherefore he arranged with Leonardo that he should enter the workshop of Andrea, which Leonardo did with the greatest willingness in the world. And he practised not one branch of art only, but all those in which drawing played a part; and having an intellect so divine and marvellous that he was also an excellent geometrician, he not only worked in sculpture, making in his youth, in clay, some heads of women that are smiling, of which plaster casts are still taken, and likewise some heads of boys which appeared to have issued from the hand of a master;[1] but in architecture, also, he made many drawings both of ground plans and of other designs of buildings; and he was the first, although but a youth, who suggested the plan of reducing the river Arno to a navigable canal from Pisa to Florence.[2] He made designs of flour mills, fulling mills, and engines that might be driven by the force of water; and since he wished that his profession should be painting, he studied much in drawing after nature, and sometimes in making models of figures in clay, over which he would lay soft pieces of cloth dipped in clay, and then set himself patiently to draw them on a certain kind of very fine Rheims cloth, or prepared linen: and he executed them in black and white with the point of his brush, so that it was a marvel, as some of them by his hand, which I have in our

1. No authenticated sculpture from this period survives 2. No building or engineering work by Leonardo survives, but there are drawings related to the Arno project, on which he in fact worked around 1503

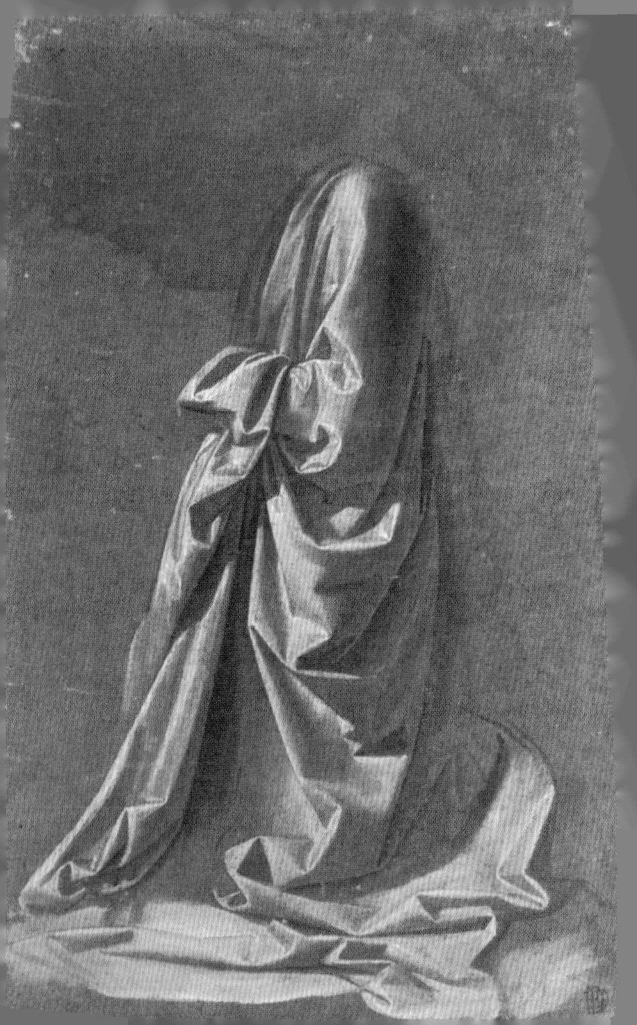

book of drawings, still bear witness;[1] besides which, he drew on paper with such diligence and so well, that there is no one who has ever equalled him in perfection of finish; and I have one, a head drawn with the style in chiaroscuro, which is divine.

And there was infused in that brain such grace from God, and a power of expression in such sublime accord with the intellect and memory that served it, and he knew so well how to express his conceptions by draughtsmanship, that he vanquished with his discourse, and confuted with his reasoning, every valiant wit. And he was continually making models and designs to show men how to remove mountains with ease, and how to bore them in order to pass from one level to another; and by means of levers, windlasses, and screws, he showed the way to raise and draw great weights, together with methods for emptying harbours, and pumps for removing water from low places, things which his brain never ceased from devising; and of these ideas and labours many drawings may be seen, scattered abroad among our craftsmen;

1. Around twenty drawings of this type and associated with Verrocchio's workshop survive, though none identifiable as from Vasari's collection; see ill. opposite

Opposite: Study of drapery for a kneeling woman, c. 1470. This drapery study on prepared linen from Verrocchio's studio is traditionally attributed to Leonardo

and I myself have seen not a few.[1] He even went so far as to waste his time in drawing knots of cords, made according to an order, that from one end all the rest might follow till the other, so as to fill a round; and one of these is to be seen in prints, most difficult and beautiful, and in the middle of it are these words, 'Leonardus Vinci Accademia'.[2] And among these models and designs, there was one by which he often demonstrated to many ingenious citizens, who were then governing Florence, how he proposed to raise the church of San Giovanni in Florence, and place steps under it, without damaging the building; and with such strong reasons did he urge this, that it appeared possible, although each man, after he had departed, would recognize for himself the impossibility of so vast an undertaking.

He was so pleasing in conversation, that he attracted to himself the hearts of men. And although he possessed, one might say, nothing, and worked little, he always kept servants and horses, in which latter

1. Approximately 5,000 pages of notes and drawings by Leonardo survive in the form of his notebooks, with major holdings at the Pinacoteca Ambrosiano, Milan; the Bibliothèque de l'Institut de France, Paris; the Victoria and Albert Museum, London; and the Royal Collection, Windsor Castle, amongst others. 2. Six knot designs were published as prints, c. 1490. See ill. p. 161.

he took much delight, and particularly in all other animals, which he managed with the greatest love and patience; and this he showed often when passing by the places where birds were sold, for, taking them with his own hand out of their cages, and having paid those who sold them the price that was asked, he let them fly away into the air, restoring to them their lost liberty. For which reason nature was pleased so to favour him, that, wherever he turned his thought, brain, and mind, he displayed such divine power in his works, that, in giving them their perfection, no one was ever his peer in readiness, vivacity, excellence, beauty, and grace.

It is clear that Leonardo, through his comprehension of art, began many things and never finished one of them, since it seemed to him that the hand was not able to attain to the perfection of art in carrying out the things which he imagined; for the reason that he conceived in his mind difficulties so subtle and so marvellous, that they could never be expressed by the hands, be they ever so excellent. And so many were his caprices, that, philosophizing of natural things, he set himself to seek out the properties of herbs, going on even to observe the motions of the heavens, the path of the moon, and the courses of the sun.

He was placed, then, as has been said, in his

boyhood, at the instance of Ser Piero, to learn art with Andrea del Verrocchio, who was making a panel-picture of St John baptizing Christ, when Leonardo painted an angel who was holding some garments; and although he was but a lad, Leonardo executed it in such a manner that his angel was much better than the figures of Andrea; which was the reason that Andrea would never again touch colour, in disdain that a child should know more than he.[1]

He was commissioned to make a cartoon for a door-hanging that was to be executed in Flanders, woven in gold and silk, to be sent to the King of Portugal, of Adam and Eve sinning in the Earthly Paradise; wherein Leonardo drew with the brush in chiaroscuro, with the lights in lead-white, a meadow of infinite kinds of herbage, with some animals, of which, in truth, it may be said that for diligence and truth to nature divine wit could not make it so perfect.[2] In it is the fig tree, together with the foreshortening of the leaves and the varying aspects of the branches, wrought with such lovingness that the brain reels at the mere thought of how a man could have

1. c. 1475, Florence, Uffizi 2. Lost

Opposite: Andrea del Verrocchio with Leonardo, The Baptism, c. 1475. Leonardo may have contributed to the landscape and figure of Christ as well as painting the angel to the far left

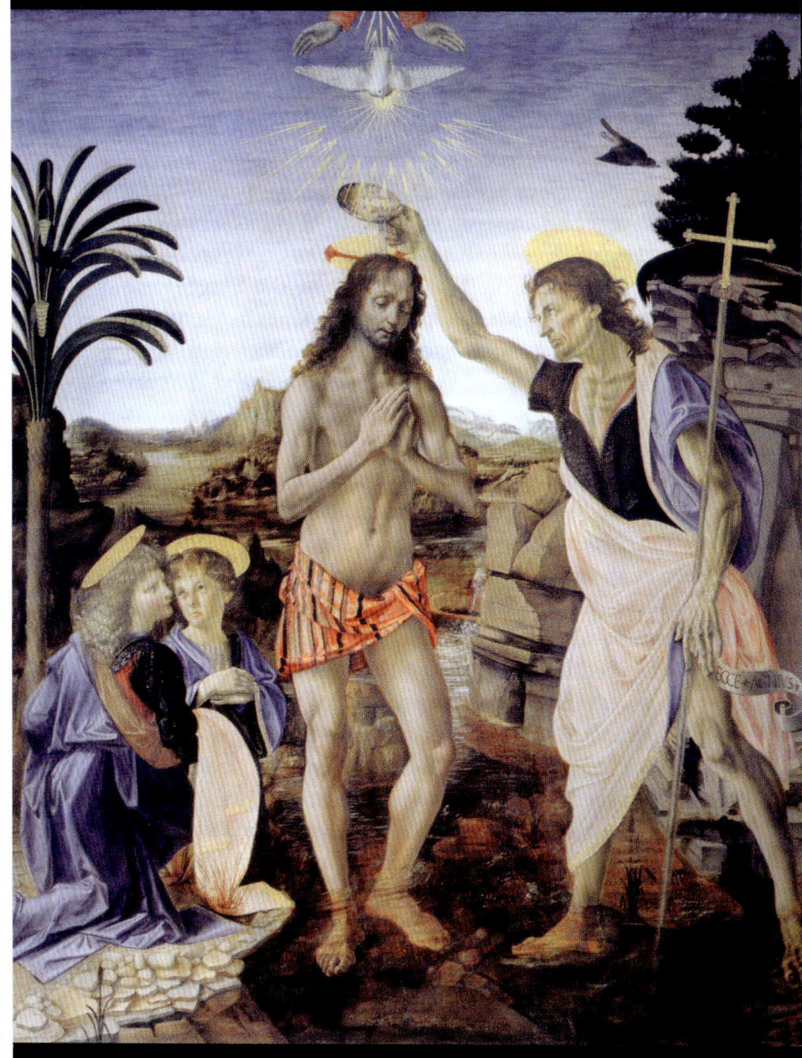

put to the window, in order to make a soft light, and then he bade him come in to see it. Ser Piero, at the first glance, taken by surprise, gave a sudden start, not thinking that that was the buckler, nor merely painted the form that he saw upon it, and, falling back a step, Leonardo checked him, saying, 'This work serves the end for which it was made; take it, then, and carry it away, since this is the effect that it was meant to produce.' This thing appeared to Ser Piero nothing short of a miracle, and he praised very greatly the ingenious idea of Leonardo; and then, having privately bought from a pedlar another buckler, painted with a heart transfixed by an arrow, he presented it to the countryman, who remained obliged to him for it as long as he lived. Afterwards, Ser Piero sold the buckler of Leonardo secretly to some merchants in Florence, for a hundred ducats; and in a short time it came into the hands of the Duke of Milan, having been sold to him by the said merchants for three hundred ducats.[1]

Leonardo then made a picture of Our Lady, a most excellent work, which was in the possession of Pope Clement VII;[2] and, among other things painted therein, he counterfeited a glass vase full of water,

1. Lost 2. Probably the *Madonna of the Carnation*, Munich, Alte Pinakothek, Munich, c. 1478-80, ill. opposite

Opposite: Madonna of the Carnation, c. 1478-80

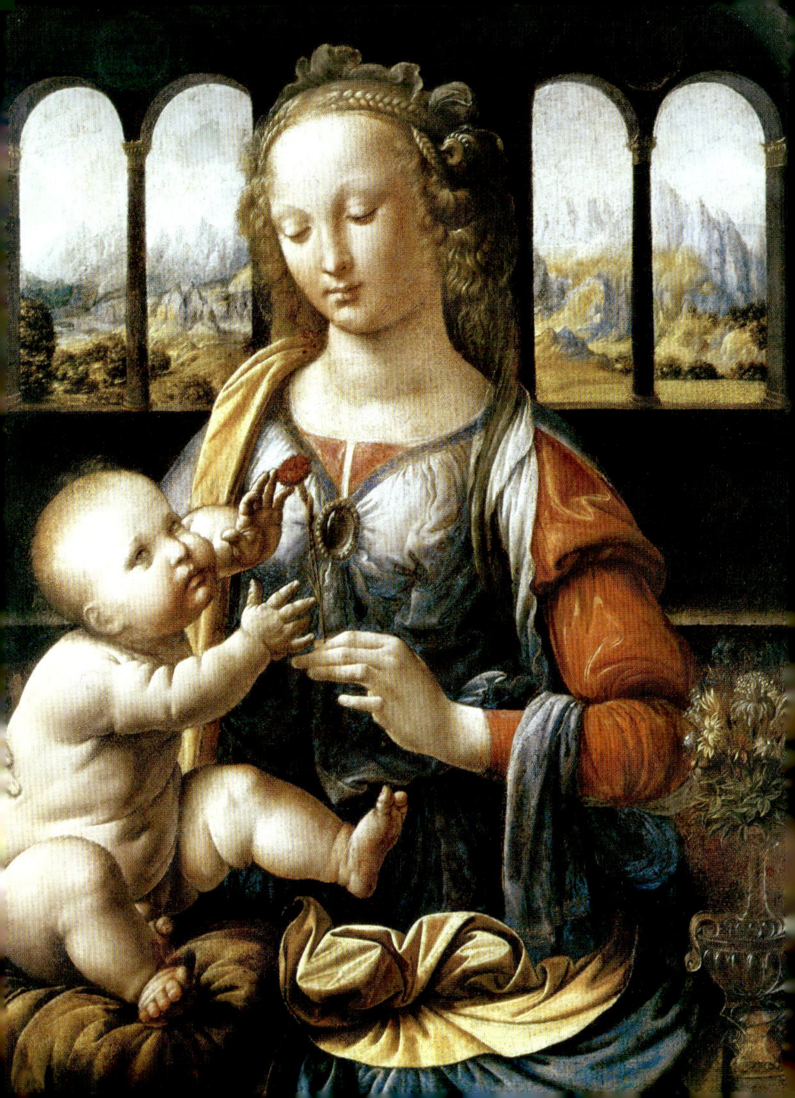

containing some flowers, in which, besides its marvellous naturalness, he had imitated the dew-drops on the flowers, so that it seemed more real than the reality. For Antonio Segni, who was very much his friend, he made, on a sheet of paper, a Neptune executed with such careful draughtsmanship that it seemed absolutely alive. In it one saw the ocean troubled, and Neptune's car drawn by sea-horses, with fantastic creatures, marine monsters and winds, and some very beautiful heads of sea-gods.[1] This drawing was presented by Fabio, the son of Antonio, to Messer Giovanni Gaddi, with this epigram:

Pinxit Virgilius Neptunum, pinxit Homerus,
Dum maris undisoni per vada flectit equos.
Mente quidem vates illum conspexit uterque,
Vincius ast oculis; jureque vincit eos.*

The fancy came to him to paint a picture in oils of the head of a Medusa, with the head attired with a coil of snakes, the most strange and extravagant

*Virgil and Homer both depicted Neptune driving his sea-horses through the rushing waves. The poets saw him in their imaginations, but da Vinci with his own eyes, and so he rightly vanquished ('vincit') them.

1. Lost. A preparatory drawing survives in the Royal Collection, Windsor

invention that could ever be imagined; but since it was a work that took time, it remained unfinished, as happened with almost all his things.[1] It is among the rare works of art in the palace of Duke Cosimo, together with the head of an angel, who is raising one arm in the air, which, coming forward, is foreshortened from the shoulder to the elbow, and with the other he raises the hand to the breast.[2]

It is an extraordinary thing how that genius, in his desire to give the highest relief to the works that he made, went so far with dark shadows, in order to find the darkest possible grounds, that he sought for blacks which might make deeper shadows and be darker than other blacks, that by their means he might make his lights the brighter; and in the end this method turned out so dark, that, no light remaining there, his pictures had rather the character of things made to represent an effect of night than the clear quality of daylight; which all came from seeking to give greater relief, and to achieve the final perfection of art.

He was so delighted when he saw certain bizarre heads of men, with the beard or hair growing naturally, that he would follow one that pleased him a whole day, and so treasured him up in his mind, that afterwards, on arriving home, he drew him as if he had

1. Lost. 2. Lost

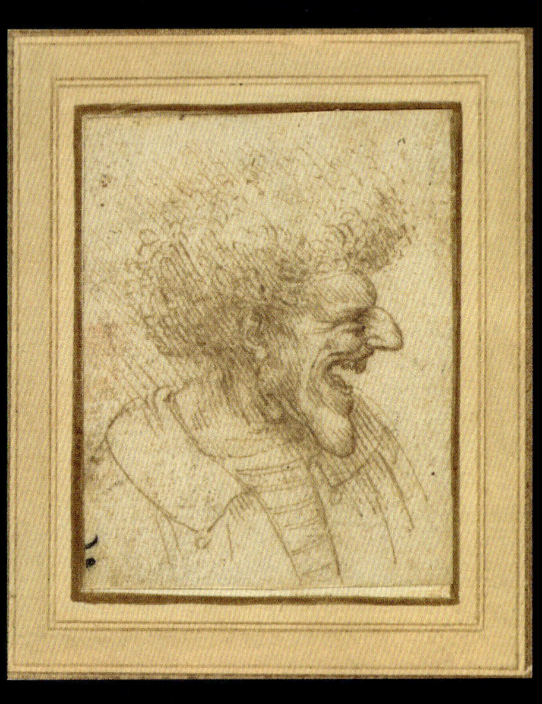

Caricature of a man with bushy hair, c. 1495
Shown approximately actual size

had him in his presence. Of this sort there are many heads to be seen, both of women and of men, and I have several of them, drawn by his hand with the pen, in our book of drawings, which I have mentioned so many times; such was that of Amerigo Vespucci, which is a very beautiful head of an old man drawn with charcoal, and likewise that of Scaramuccia, Captain of the Gypsies, which afterwards came into the hands of M. Donato Valdambrini of Arezzo, Canon of S. Lorenzo, left to him by Giambullari.[1]

He began a panel-picture of the Adoration of the Magi, containing many beautiful things, particularly the heads, which was in the house of Amerigo Benci, opposite the Loggia de' Peruzzi; and this, also, remained unfinished, like his other works.[2]

It came to pass that Giovan Galeazzo, Duke of Milan, being dead, and Lodovico Sforza raised to the same rank, in the year 1494, Leonardo, whose reputation was great, was sent to Milan to the Duke, who took much delight in the sound of the lyre, to the end that he might play it: and Leonardo took with him an instrument that he had made with his own hands, in great part of silver, in the form of a horse's skull – a thing bizarre and new – in order that the harmony

1. Drawings unidentified. 2. 1480-81, The underdrawing is by Leonardo but areas of paint possibly by other hands. Uffizi, Florence.

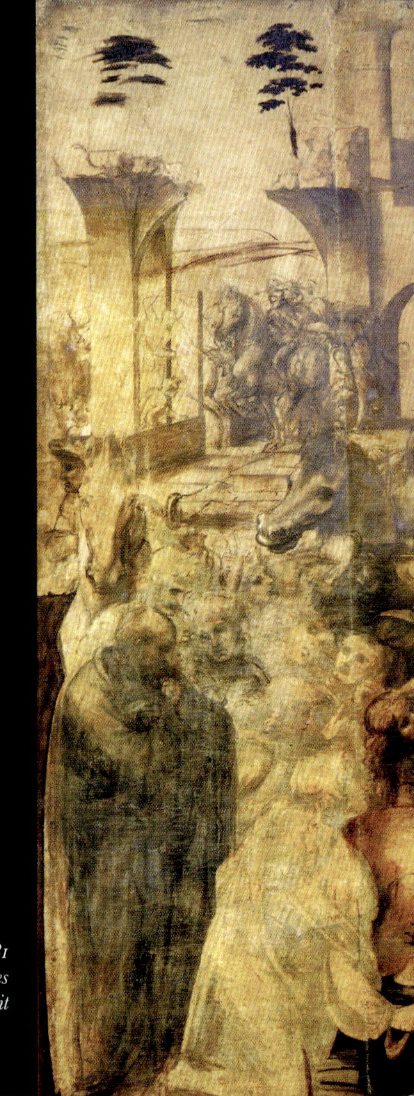

The Adoration of the Magi, 1480-81
The figure on the far right is sometimes thought to be a self-portrait

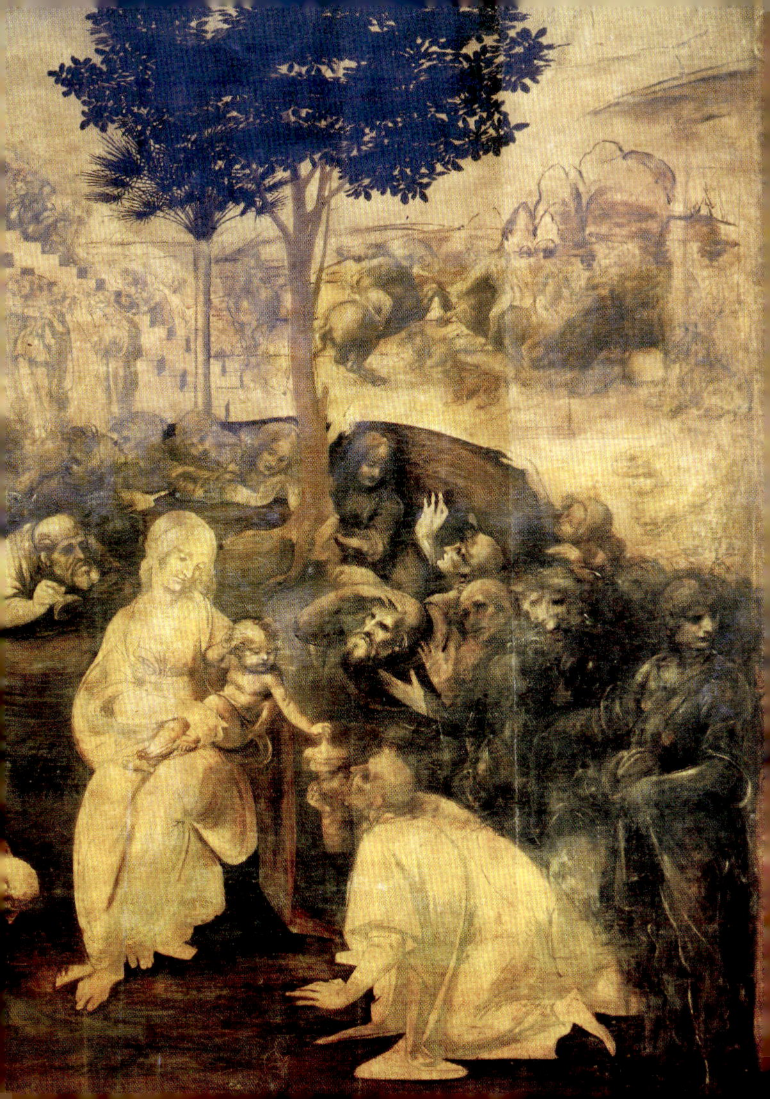

might be of greater volume and more sonorous in tone; with which he surpassed all the musicians who had come together there to play.[1]

Besides this, he was the best improviser in verse of his day. The Duke, hearing the marvellous discourse of Leonardo, became so enamoured of his genius, that it was something incredible: and he prevailed upon him by entreaties to paint an altar-panel containing a Nativity, which was sent by the Duke to the Emperor.[2]

He also painted in Milan, for the Friars of S. Dominic, at S. Maria delle Grazie, a Last Supper,[3] a most beautiful and marvellous thing; and to the heads of the Apostles he gave such majesty and beauty, that he left the head of Christ unfinished, not believing that he was able to give it that divine air which is essential to the image of Christ. This work, remaining thus all but finished, has ever been held by the Milanese in the greatest veneration, and also by strangers as well; for Leonardo imagined and succeeded in expressing that anxiety which had seized the Apostles in wishing to know who should betray their Master. For which reason in all their faces are seen love, fear, and wrath,

1. Lost 2. Possibly one of the two versions of the Virgin of the Rocks, see ill. p. 111 3. 1495-98, still in situ, see ill. in foldout pp. 58-60.

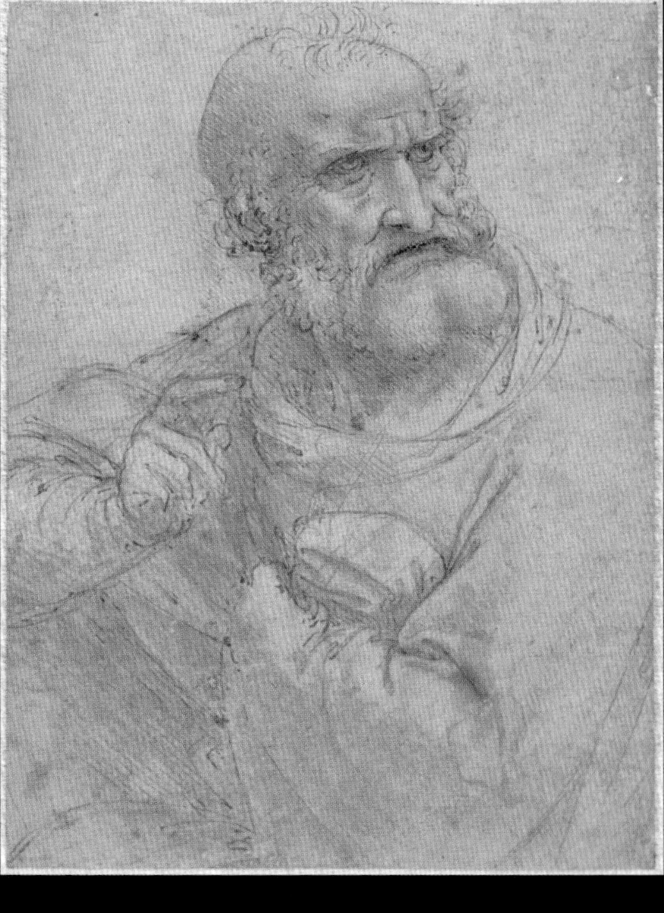

Half-length figure of an apostle, 1493-95: : a study for the Last Supper

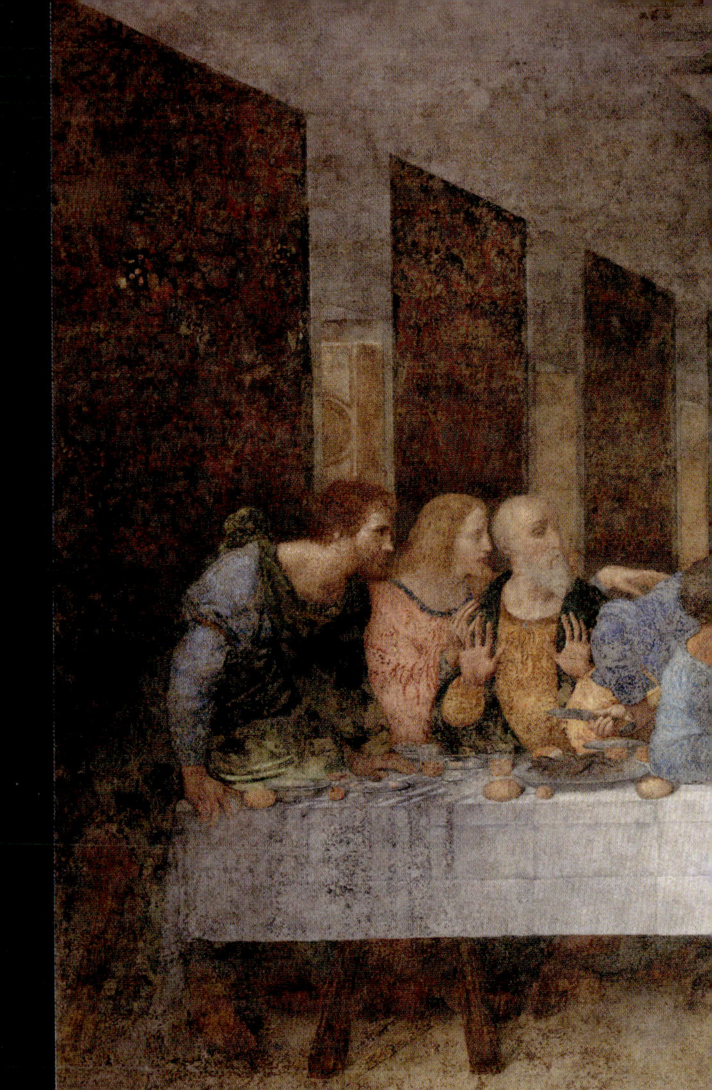

In about 1493-98, Leonardo made notes about the reactions and gestures of a group of men at dinner, as part of his preparations for the Last Supper*:*

One who was drinking and has left the glass in its place and turned his head towards the speaker. Another, twisting the fingers of his hands together, turns with stern brow to his companion. Another with his hands spread open shows the palms, and shrugs his shoulders up to his ears, making a mouth of astonishment. Another speaks into his neighbour's ear and he, as he listens to him, turns towards him to lend an ear, while he holds a knife in one hand, and in the other the loaf half cut through by the knife. Another who has turned, holding a knife in his hand, upsets with his hand a glass onto the table. Another lays his hands on the table and is looking. Another blows his mouthful. Another leans forward to see the speaker, shading his eyes with his hand. Another draws back behind the one who leans forward, and sees the speaker between the wall and the man who is leaning.

☛ *Fold-out: The Last Supper, 1495-98*

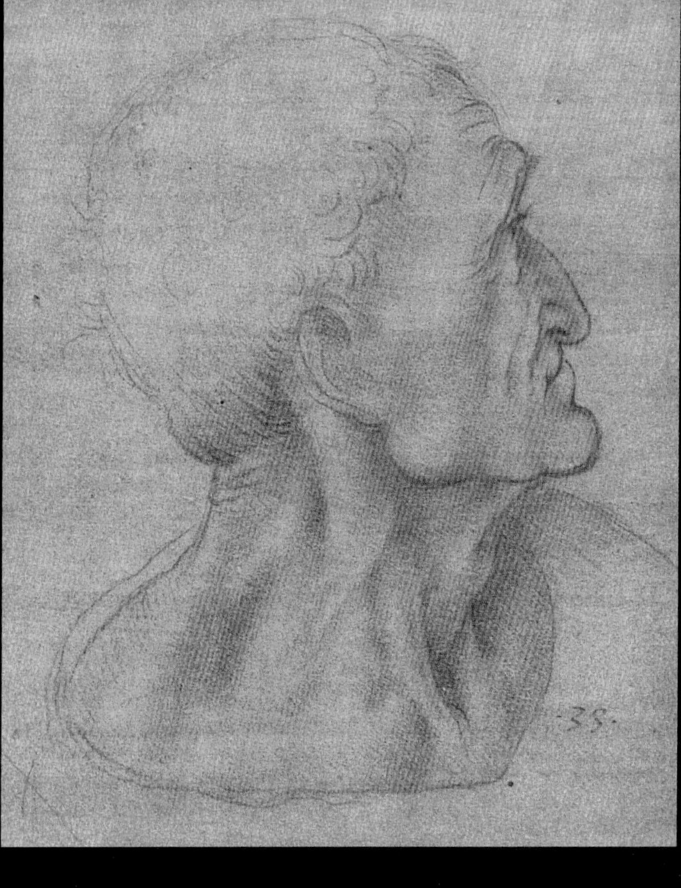

Had of Judas, 1493-95: a study for the Last Supper

or rather, sorrow, at not being able to understand the meaning of Christ; which thing excites no less marvel than the sight, in contrast to it, of obstinacy, hatred, and treachery in Judas; not to mention that every least part of the work displays an incredible diligence, seeing that even in the tablecloth the texture of the stuff is counterfeited in such a manner that linen itself could not seem more real.

It is said that the Prior of that place kept pressing Leonardo, in a most importunate manner, to finish the work; for it seemed strange to him to see Leonardo sometimes stand half a day at a time, lost in contemplation, and he would have liked him to go on like the labourers hoeing in his garden, without ever stopping his brush. And not content with this, he complained of it to the Duke, and that so warmly, that he was constrained to send for Leonardo and delicately urged him to work, contriving nevertheless to show him that he was doing all this because of the importunity of the Prior. Leonardo, knowing that the intellect of that Prince was acute and discerning, was pleased to discourse at large with the Duke on the subject, a thing which he had never done with the Prior: and he reasoned much with him about art, and made him understand that men of lofty genius sometimes accomplish the most when they work the least, seeking out inventions with the mind, and forming those perfect ideas which the hands afterwards express and reproduce from the images already conceived in the brain. And he added that there were two heads he still had not painted: that of Christ, which he did not wish to seek on earth; and he could not think that it was possible to conceive in the imagination that beauty and heavenly grace which should be the mark of God incarnate; and next, that of Judas, which was also troubling him, as he did not think himself capable of imagining features that should represent the countenance of him who, after so many benefits received, had a mind so cruel as to resolve to betray his Lord, the Creator of the world. However, he would seek out a model for the latter; but if in the end he could not find a better, he could at least use that of the importunate and tactless Prior. This thing moved the Duke wondrously to laughter, and he said that Leonardo had a thousand reasons on his side. And so the poor Prior, in confusion, confined himself to urging on the work in the garden, and left Leonardo in peace, who finished only the head of Judas, which seems the very embodiment of treachery and inhumanity; but that of Christ, as has been said, remained unfinished. The nobility of this picture, both because of its design, and from its having been wrought with an incomparable diligence, awoke a desire in the King of France to transport it into his kingdom; wherefore he tried by all possible means to discover whether there were architects who, with cross-stays of wood and iron, might have been able to make it so secure that it might be transported safely; without considering any expense that might have been involved, so much did he desire it. But the fact of its being painted on the wall robbed his Majesty of his desire; and the picture remained with the Milanese. In the same refectory, while he was working at the Last Supper, on the end wall where is a Passion in the old manner, Leonardo portrayed the said Lodovico, with Massimiliano, his eldest son; and, on the other side, the Duchess Beatrice, with Francesco, their other son, both of whom afterwards became Dukes of Milan; and all are portrayed divinely well.[1]

While he was engaged on this work, he proposed to the Duke to make a horse in bronze, of a marvellous greatness, in order to place upon it, as a memorial, the image of the Duke. And on so vast a scale did he begin it and continue it, that it could never be completed. And there are those who have been of the opinion (so various and so often malign out of envy are the

1. Still in situ, but badly damaged. Possibly by an assistant

judgments of men) that he began it with no intention of finishing it, because, being of so great a size, an incredible difficulty was encountered in seeking to cast it in one piece; and it might also be believed that, from the result, many may have formed such a judgment, since many of his works have remained unfinished. But, in truth, one can believe that his vast and most excellent mind was hampered through being too full of desire, and that his wish ever to seek out excellence upon excellence, and perfection upon perfection, was the reason of it. 'Such that the work was delayed by the desire,' as our Petrarch has said. And, indeed, those who saw the great model that Leonardo made in clay vow that they have never seen a more beautiful thing, or a more superb; and it was preserved until the French came to Milan with King Louis of France, and broke it all to pieces. Lost, also, is a little model of it in wax, which was held to be perfect, together with a book on the anatomy of the horse made by him by way of study.

He then applied himself, but with greater care, to the anatomy of man, assisted by and in turn assisting in this research, Messer Marc' Antonio della Torre, an excellent philosopher, who was then lecturing at Pavia, and who wrote of this matter; and he was one of the first (as I have heard tell) that began to illustrate

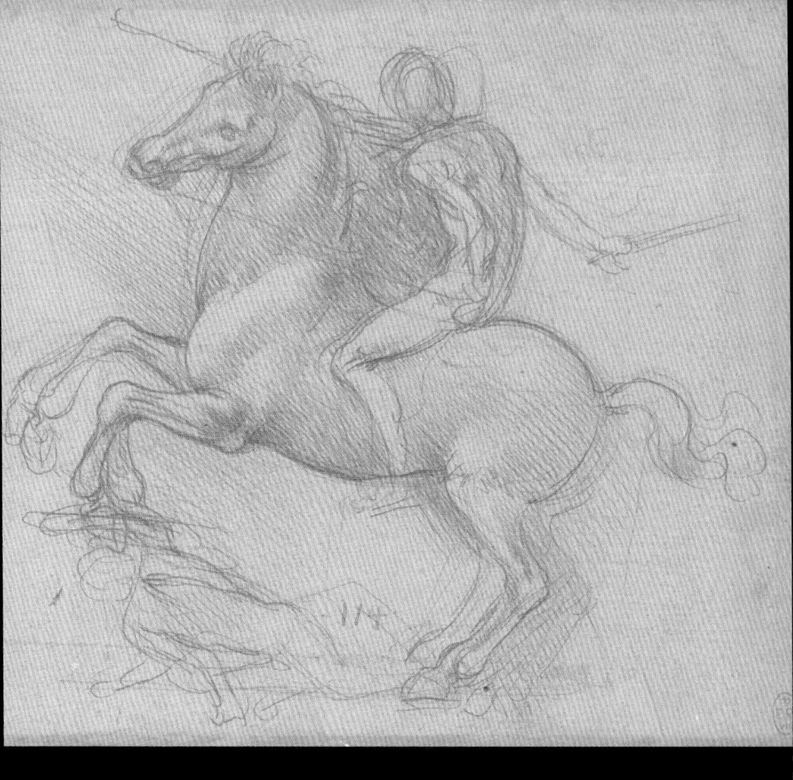

Study for an equestrian monument, c. 1485-90

the problems of medicine with the doctrine of Galen, and to throw true light on anatomy, which up to that time had been wrapped in the thick and gross darkness of ignorance. And in this he found marvellous aid in the brain, work, and hand of Leonardo, who made a book drawn in red chalk, and annotated with the pen, of the bodies that he dissected with his own hand, and drew with the greatest diligence; wherein he showed all the frame of the bones; and then added to them, in order, all the nerves, and covered them with muscles; the first attached to the bone, the second that hold the body firm, and the third that move it; and beside them, part by part, he wrote in letters of an ill-shaped character, which he made with the left hand, backwards; and whoever is not practised in reading them cannot understand them, since they are not to be read save with a mirror. Of these papers on the anatomy of man, a great part is in the hands of Messer Francesco de Melzi, a gentleman of Milan, who in the time of Leonardo was a very beautiful boy, and much beloved by him, and now is a no less beautiful and gentle old man; and he holds them

Opposite: Two-sided sheet of anatomical studies, c. 1510-11.
This side (recto): the superficial anatomy of the shoulder and neck.
For other side (verso), see p. 70

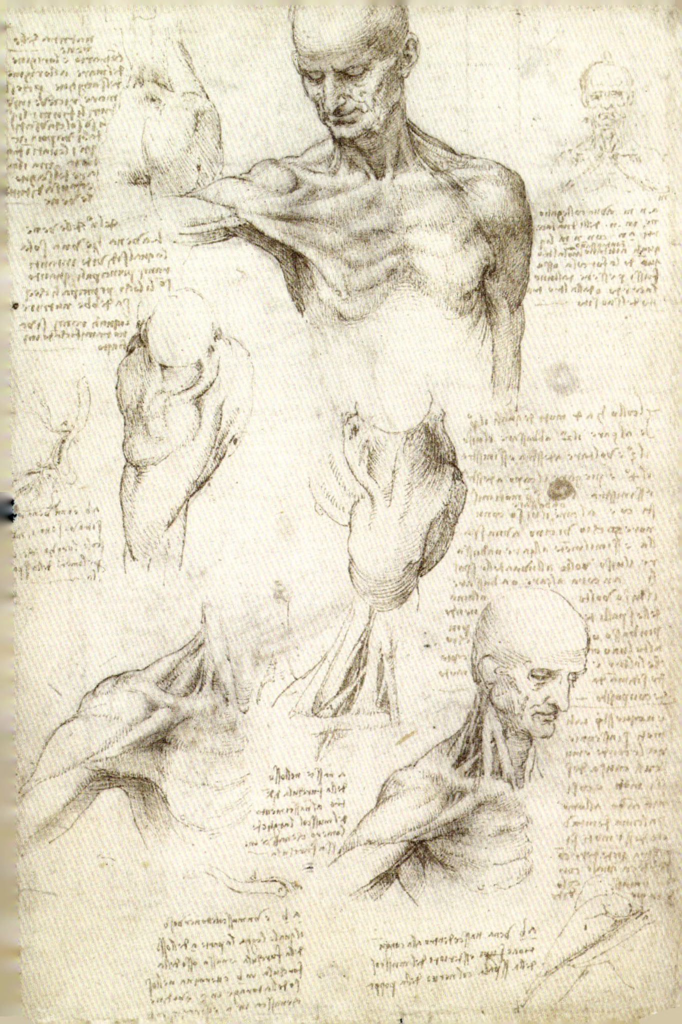

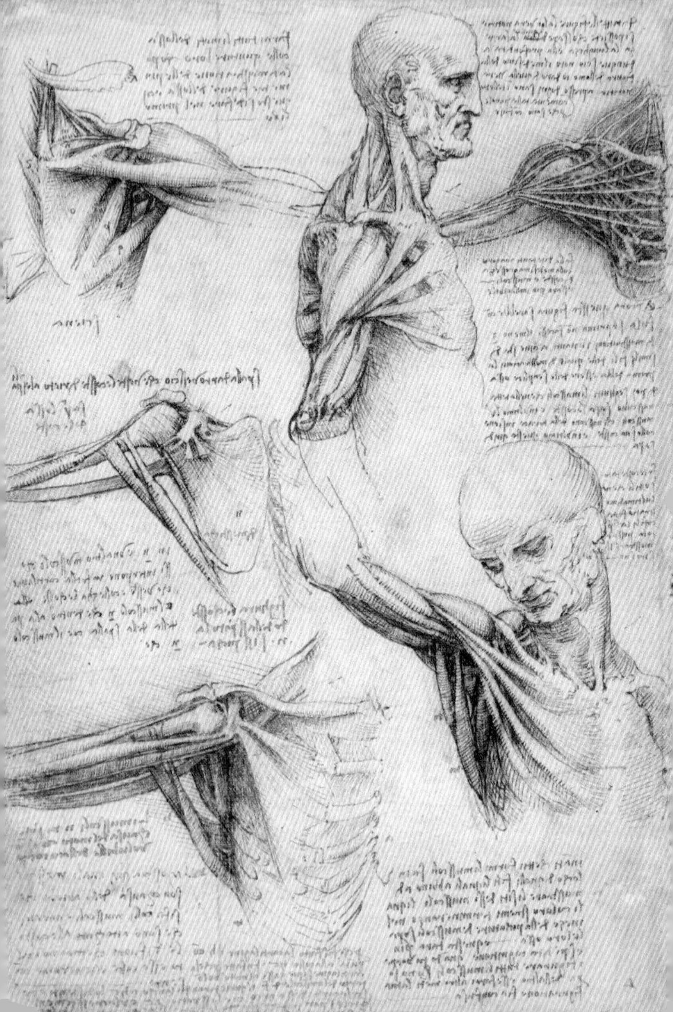

dear, and keeps such papers together as if they were relics, in company with the portrait of Leonardo of happy memory; and to all who read these writings, it seems impossible that that divine spirit should have discoursed so well of art, and of the muscles, nerves, and veins, and with such diligence of everything.[1] So, also, there are in the hands of ——, a painter of Milan, certain writings of Leonardo, likewise in characters written with the left hand, backwards, which treat of painting, and of the methods of drawing and colouring. This man, not long ago, came to Florence to see me, wishing to print this work, and he took it to Rome, in order to put it into effect; but I do not know what may afterwards have become of it.

And to return to the works of Leonardo; there came to Milan, in his time, the King of France, wherefore Leonardo being asked to devise some bizarre thing, made a lion which walked several steps and then opened its breast, and showed it full of lilies.[2]

1. The collaboration with Marc' Antonio della Torre took place during the second Milanese period, c. 1510. Melzi's collection of drawings and writings are now in the Royal Collection, and include a portrait of Leonardo, possibly by Melzi, see ill. p. 158 2. Lost

Opposite: Two-sided sheet of anatomical studies, c. 1510-11.
This side (verso): the muscles of the shoulder

In Milan he took for his assistant the Milanese Salai, who was most comely in grace and beauty, having fine locks, curling in ringlets, in which Leonardo greatly delighted; and he taught him many things of art; and certain works in Milan, which are said to be by Salai, were retouched by Leonardo.

He returned to Florence, where he found that the Servite Friars had entrusted to Filippino the painting of the panel for the high altar of the Nunziata; whereupon Leonardo said that he would willingly have done such a work. Filippino, having heard this, like the amiable fellow that he was, retired from the undertaking; and the friars, to the end that Leonardo might paint it, took him into their house, meeting the expenses both of himself and of all his household; and thus he kept them in expectation for a long time, but never began anything. In the end, he made a cartoon containing a Madonna and a St Anne, with a Christ, which not only caused all the craftsmen to marvel, but, when it was finished, men and women, young and old, continued for two days to flock for a sight of it to the room where it was, as if to a solemn festival, in order to gaze at the marvels of Leonardo,

Opposite: Head of a youth, c. 1510-11. This type, frequently drawn by Leonardo, is sometimes thought to represent his assistant Salai

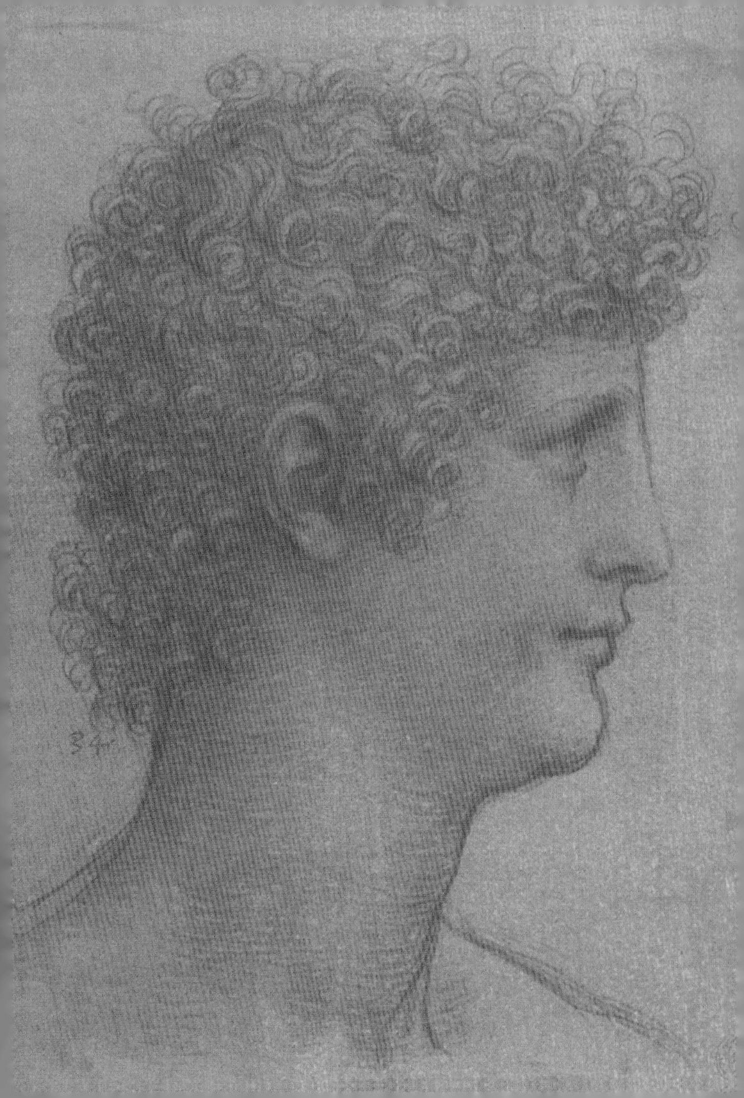

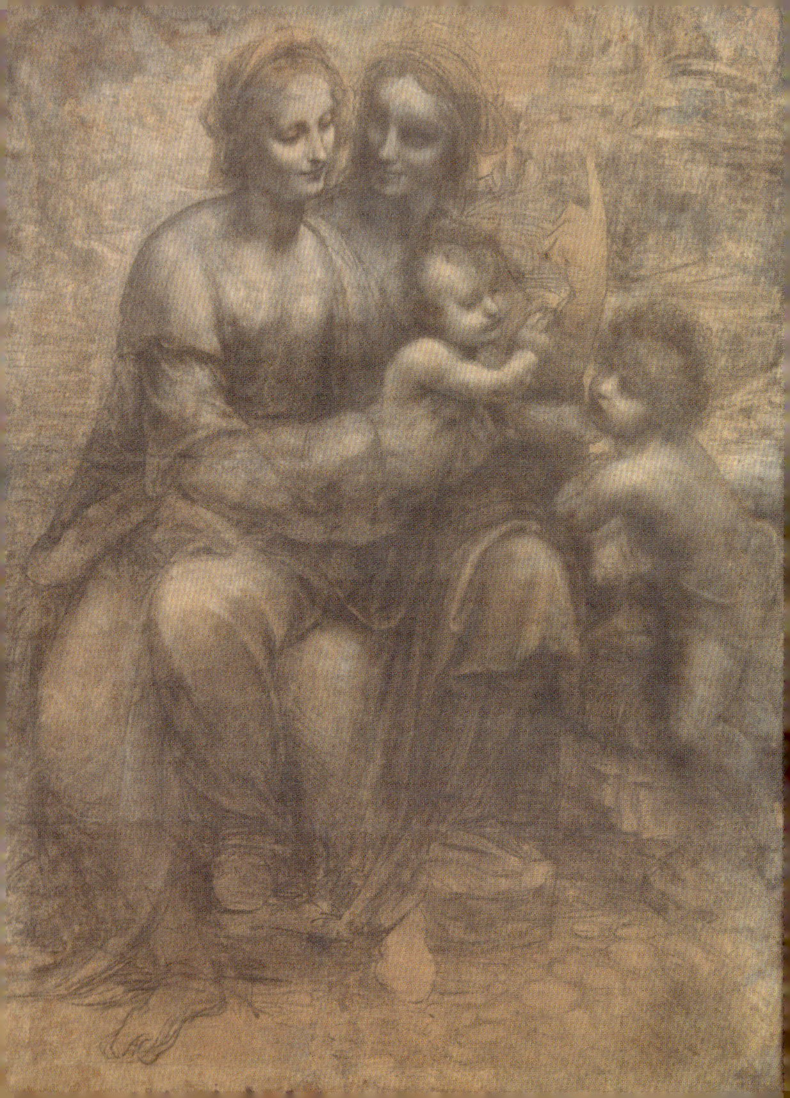

which caused all those people to be amazed; for in the face of that Madonna was seen whatever of the simple and the beautiful can by simplicity and beauty confer grace on a picture of the Mother of Christ, since he wished to show that modesty and that humility which are looked for in an image of the Virgin, supremely content with gladness at seeing the beauty of her Son, whom she was holding with tenderness in her lap, while with most chastened gaze she was looking down at St John, as a little boy, who was playing with a lamb; not without a smile from St Anne, who, overflowing with joy, was beholding her earthly progeny become divine – ideas truly worthy of the brain and genius of Leonardo.[1] This cartoon, as will be told below, afterwards went to France. He made a portrait of Ginevra d'Amerigo Benci, a very beautiful work;[2] and abandoned the work for the friars, who restored it to Filippino; but he, too, failed to finish it, having been overtaken by death.

1. Lost, but compare with the Burlington House Cartoon, ill. opposite. It is possible that this is the drawing intended by Vasari but that he was confused in his description 2. c. 1478, Washington, DC, National Gallery of Art, ill. p. 107

Opposite: The Virgin and Child with St Anne and the infant St John the Baptist (known as the Burlington House Cartoon), c. 1499-1500

Leonardo undertook to execute, for Francesco del Giocondo, the portrait of Mona Lisa, his wife; and after toiling over it for four years, he left it unfinished; and the work is now in the collection of King Francis of France, at Fontainebleau.[1] In this head, whoever wished to see how closely art could imitate nature, was able to comprehend it with ease; for in it were counterfeited all the minutenesses that with subtlety are able to be painted, seeing that the eyes had that lustre and watery sheen which are always seen in life, and around them were all those rosy and pearly tints, as well as the lashes, which cannot be represented without the greatest subtlety. The eyebrows, through his having shown the manner in which the hairs spring from the flesh, here more close and here more scanty, and curve according to the pores of the skin, could not be more natural. The nose, with its beautiful nostrils, rosy and tender, appeared to be alive. The mouth, with its opening, and with its ends united by the red of the lips to the flesh-tints of the face, seemed, in truth, to be not colours but flesh. In the pit

1. c. 1503-17, Paris, Louvre; ill. opposite and on p. 78. It is likely however that Vasari did not see this version, but the one painted by assistants and now in the Prado, ill. p. 26; see introduction

Opposite: Mona Lisa (detail), c. 1503-17

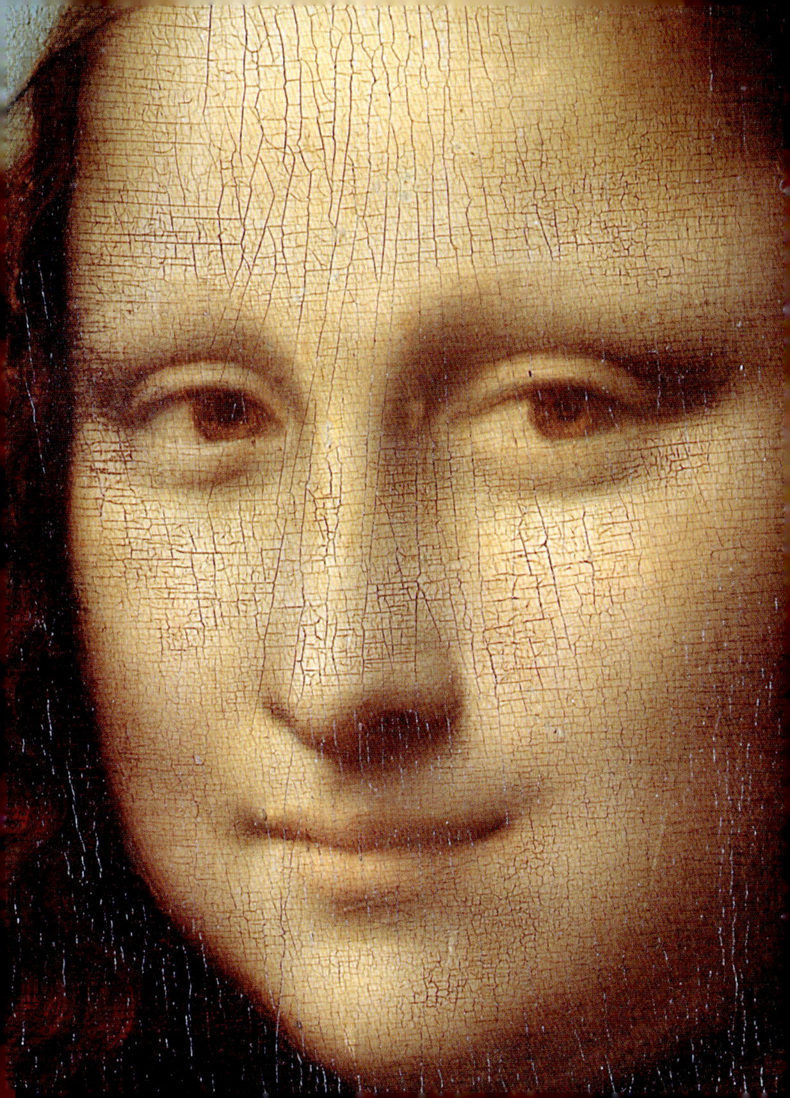

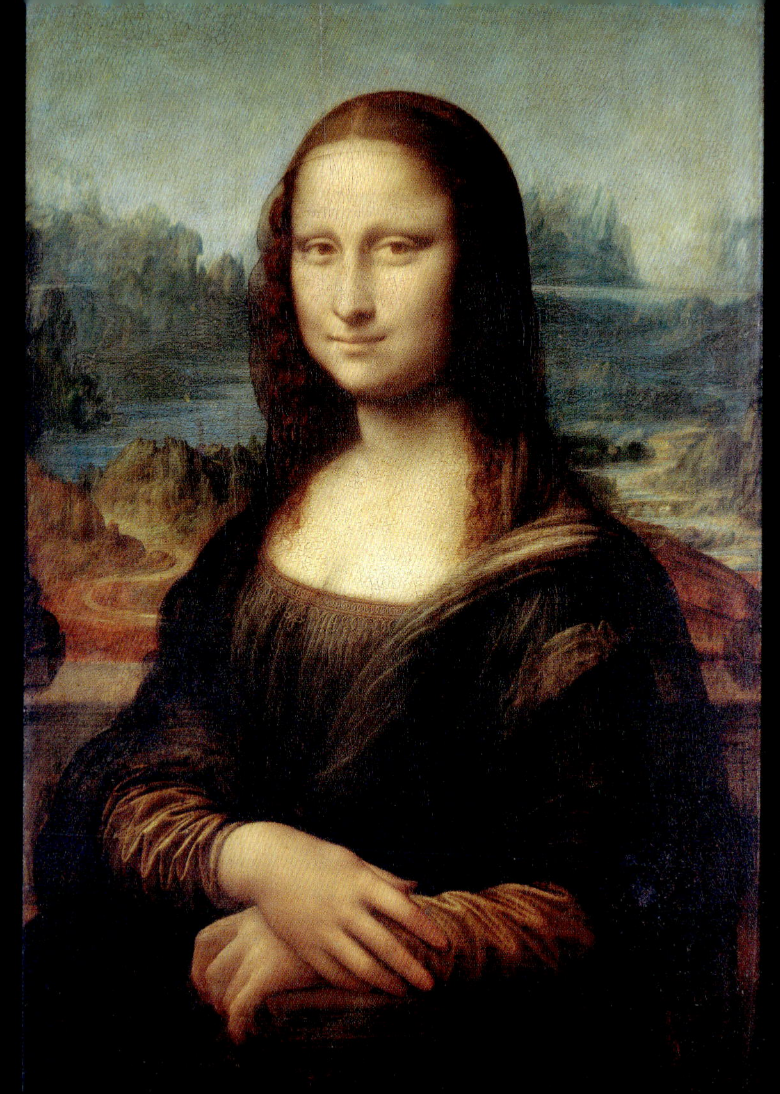

of the throat, if one gazed upon it intently, could be seen the beating of the pulse. And, indeed, it may be said that it was painted in such a manner as to make every valiant craftsman, be he who he may, tremble and lose heart. He made use, also, of this device: Mona Lisa being very beautiful, he always employed, while he was painting her portrait, persons to play or sing, and jesters, who might make her remain merry, in order to take away that melancholy which painters are often wont to give to the portraits that they paint. And in this work of Leonardo's there was a smile so pleasing, that it was a thing more divine than human to behold; and it was held to be something marvellous, since the reality was not more alive.

By reason, then, of the excellence of the works of this most divine craftsman, his fame had so increased that all persons who took delight in art – nay, the whole city of Florence – desired that he should leave them some memorial, and it was being proposed everywhere that he should be commissioned to execute some great and notable work, whereby the commonwealth might be honoured and adorned by the great genius, grace and judgment that were seen in the works of Leonardo. And it was decided

Opposite: Mona Lisa, c. 1503-17

between the Gonfalonier and the chief citizens, the Great Council Chamber having been newly built – the architecture of which had been contrived with the judgment and counsel of Giuliano da San Gallo, Simone Pollaiuolo, called Il Cronaca, Michelagnolo Buonarroti, and Baccio d'Agnolo, as will be related with more detail in the proper places – and having been finished in great haste, it was ordained by public decree that Leonardo should be given some beautiful work to paint; and so the said hall was allotted to him by Piero Soderini, then Gonfalonier of Justice. Whereupon Leonardo, determining to execute this work, began a cartoon in the Sala del Papa, an apartment in Santa Maria Novella, representing the story of Niccolò Piccinino, Captain of Duke Filippo of Milan; wherein he designed a group of horsemen who were fighting for a standard, a work that was held to be very excellent and of great mastery, by reason of the marvellous ideas that he had in composing that battle; seeing that in it rage, fury, and revenge are perceived as much in the men as in the horses, among which two with the fore-legs interlocked are fighting no less fiercely with their teeth than those who are riding them do in fighting for that standard, which has been grasped by a soldier, who seeks by the strength of his shoulders, as he spurs his horse to flight, having

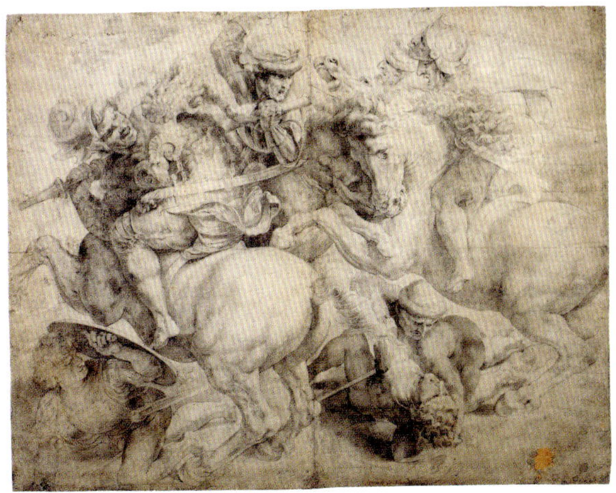

Unknown artist, Drawing after the Battle of Anghiari, 16th century

turned his body backwards and seized the staff of the standard, to wrest it by force from the hands of four others, of whom two are defending it, each with one hand, and, raising their swords in the other, are trying to sever the staff; while an old soldier in a red cap, crying out, grips the staff with one hand, and, raising a scimitar with the other, furiously aims a blow in order to cut off both the hands of those who, gnashing their teeth in the struggle, are striving in attitudes of

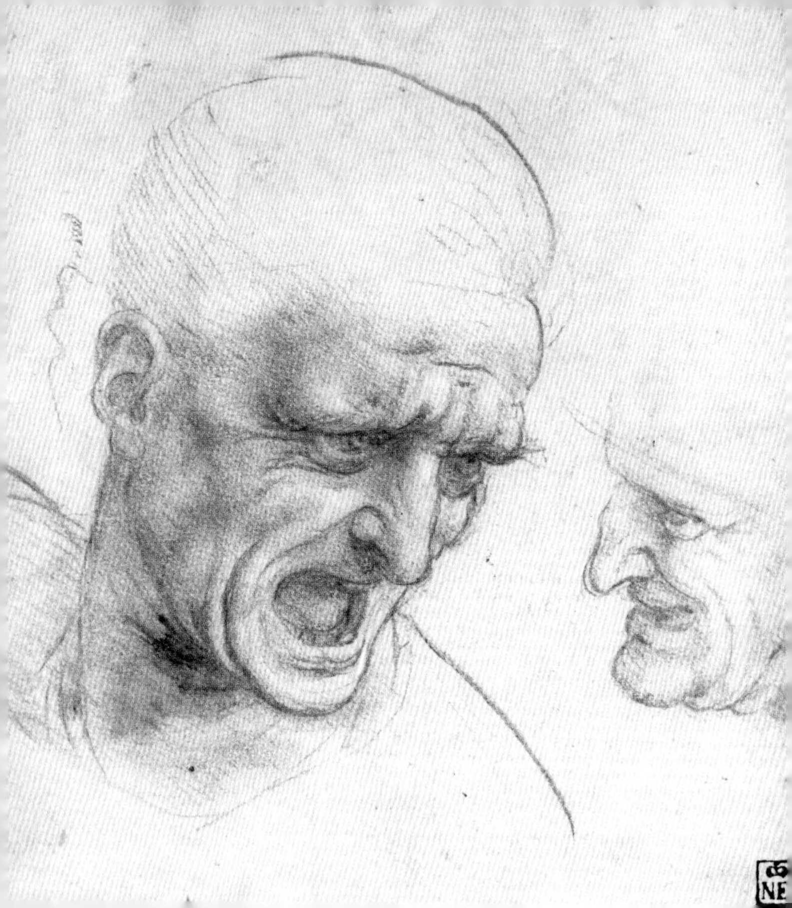

the utmost fierceness to defend their banner; besides which, on the ground, between the legs of the horses, there are two figures in foreshortening also fighting together, and the one on the ground has over him a soldier who has raised his arm as high as possible, that thus with greater force he may plunge a dagger into his throat, in order to end his life; while the other, struggling with his legs and arms, is doing what he can to escape death.

It is not possible to describe the invention that Leonardo showed in the garments of the soldiers, all varied by him in different ways, and likewise in the helmet crests and other ornaments; not to mention the incredible mastery that he displayed in the forms and lineaments of the horses, which Leonardo, with their fiery spirit, muscles, and shapely beauty, drew better than any other master. It is said that, in order to draw that cartoon, he made a most ingenious stage, which was raised by contracting it and lowered by expanding. And conceiving the wish to colour on the wall in oils, he made a composition of so gross an admixture, to act as a binder on the wall, that, going on to paint in the said hall, it began to peel off in such

Opposite: Study of two warriors' heads for the Battle of Anghiari, c. 1504-5

Overleaf: Study of fury in horses, lion and man; rearing horse, c. 1503-4

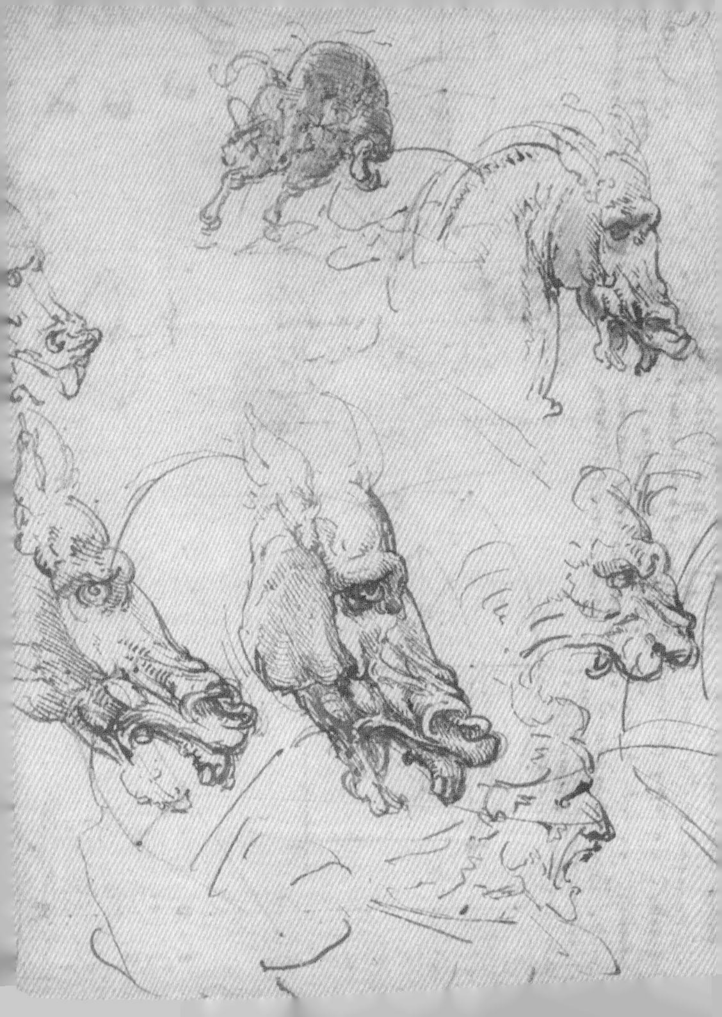

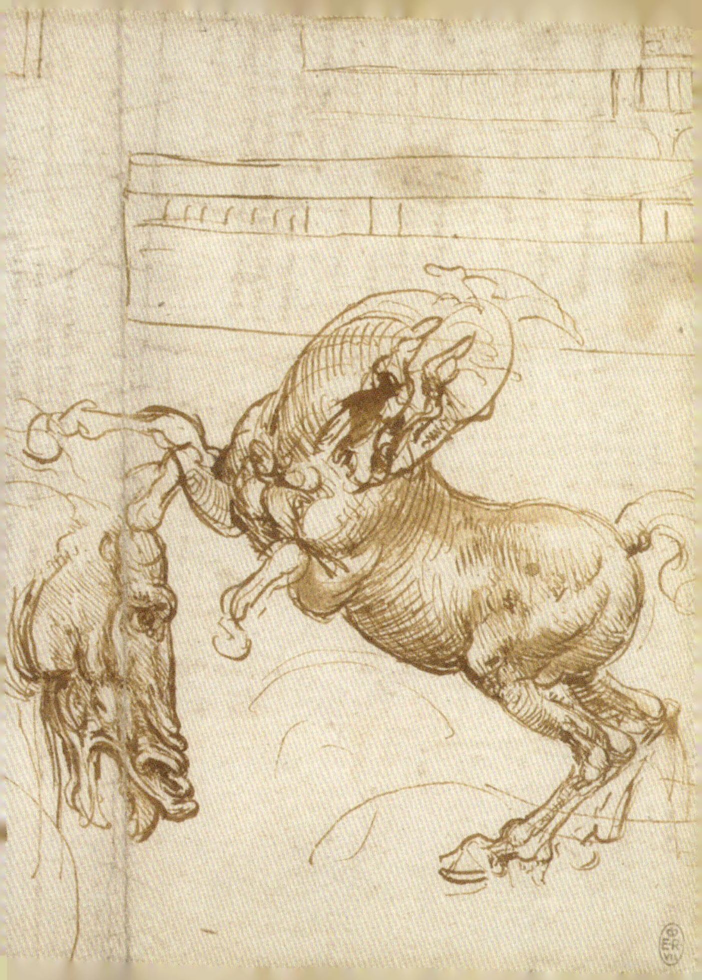

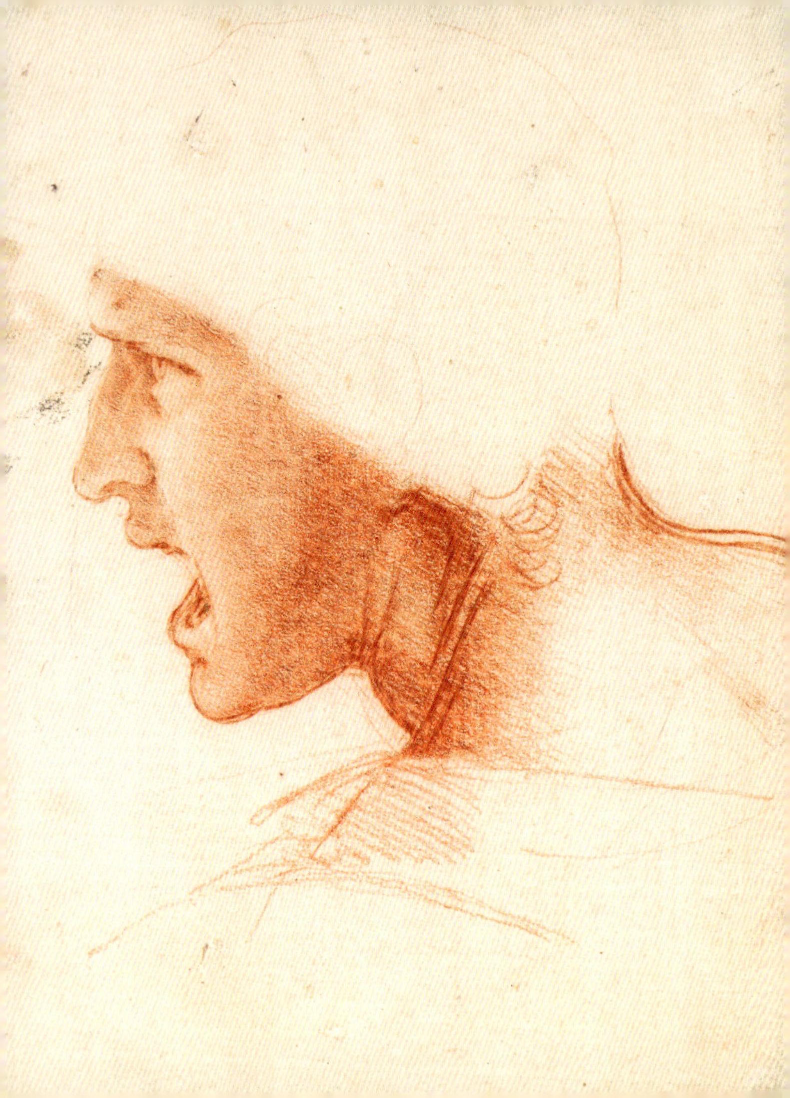

a manner that in a short time he abandoned it, seeing it spoiling.[1]

Leonardo had very great spirit, and in his every action was most generous. It is said that, going to the bank for the allowance that he used to draw every month from Piero Soderini, the cashier wanted to give him certain paper-packets of pence; but he would not take them, saying in answer, 'I am no penny-painter.' Having been blamed for cheating Piero Soderini, there began to be murmurings against him; wherefore Leonardo so wrought upon his friends, that he got the money together and took it to Piero to repay him; but he would not accept it.

He went to Rome with Duke Giuliano de' Medici at the election of Pope Leo, who spent much of his time on philosophical studies, and particularly on alchemy; where, forming a paste of a certain kind of wax, as he walked he shaped animals very thin and full of wind, and, by blowing into them, made them fly through the air, but once the air had all escaped they fell to the ground. On the back of a most bizarre lizard, found by the vine-dresser of the Belvedere,

1. The cartoon was commissioned in 1503, and Leonardo worked in the hall until 1506. The painting was covered over by Vasari in 1563

Opposite: Study of warrior's head for the Battle of Anghiari, c. 1504-5

he fixed, with a mixture of quicksilver, wings composed of scales stripped from other lizards, which, as it walked, quivered with the motion; and having given it eyes, horns, and beard, taming it, and keeping it in a box, he made all his friends, to whom he showed it, fly for fear. He used often to have the guts of a wether completely freed of their fat and cleaned, and thus made so fine that they could have been held in the palm of the hand; and having placed a pair of blacksmith's bellows in another room, he fixed to them one end of these, and, blowing into them, filled the room, which was very large, so that whoever was in it was obliged to retreat into a corner; showing how, transparent and full of wind, from taking up little space at the beginning they had come to occupy much, and likening them to virtue. He made an infinite number of such follies, and gave his attention to mirrors; and he tried the strangest methods in seeking out oils for painting, and varnish for preserving works when painted.

He made at this time, for Messer Baldassarre Turini da Pescia, who was Datary to Pope Leo [X], a little picture of the Madonna with the Child in her arms, with infinite diligence and art; but whether through the fault of whoever primed the panel with gesso, or because of his innumerable and capricious mixtures

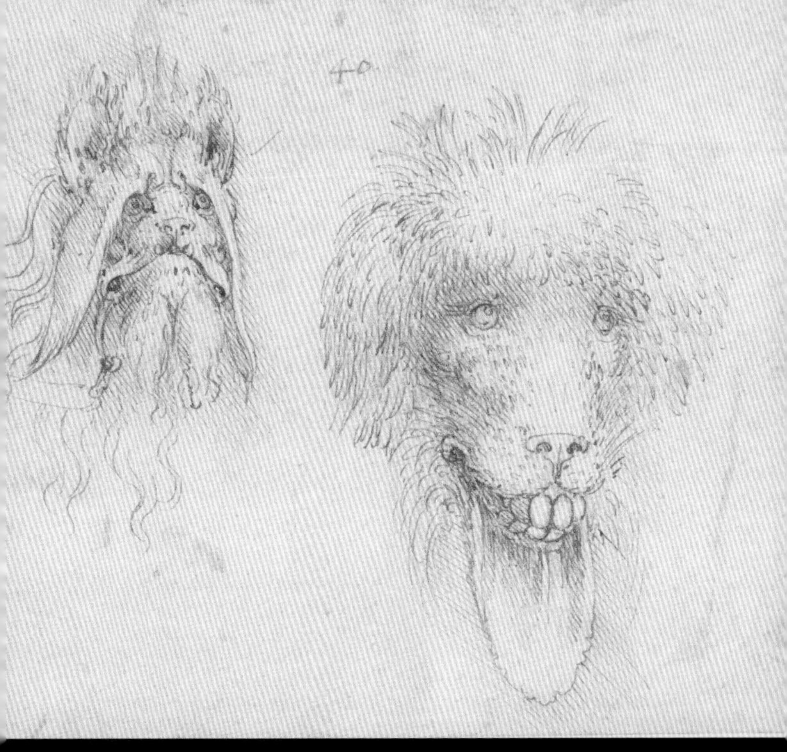

Two heads of grotesque animals, 1490-95

of grounds and colours, it is now much spoilt.[1] And in another small picture he made a portrait of a little boy, which is beautiful and graceful to a marvel;[2] and both of them are now at Pescia, in the hands of Messer Giuliano Turini. It is related that, a work having been allotted to him by the Pope, he straightway began to distil oils and herbs, in order to make the varnish; at which Pope Leo said: 'Alas! this man will never do anything, for he begins by thinking of the end of the work, before the beginning.'

There was very great disdain between Michelagnolo Buonarroti and him, on account of which Michelagnolo departed from Florence, with the excuse of Duke Giuliano, having been summoned by the Pope to the competition for the façade of San Lorenzo. Leonardo, understanding this, departed and went into France, where the King, having had works by his hand, bore him great affection; and he desired that he should colour the cartoon of St Anne, but Leonardo, according to his custom, put him off for a long time with words.

1. Lost. 2. Possibly Bernardino Luini, *Boy with a Puzzle*, c. 1515, Elton Hall, England

Opposite: Two-sided sheet of botanical studies, c. 1506-12. This side (recto), a bullrush; overleaf (verso) a branched bur-reed

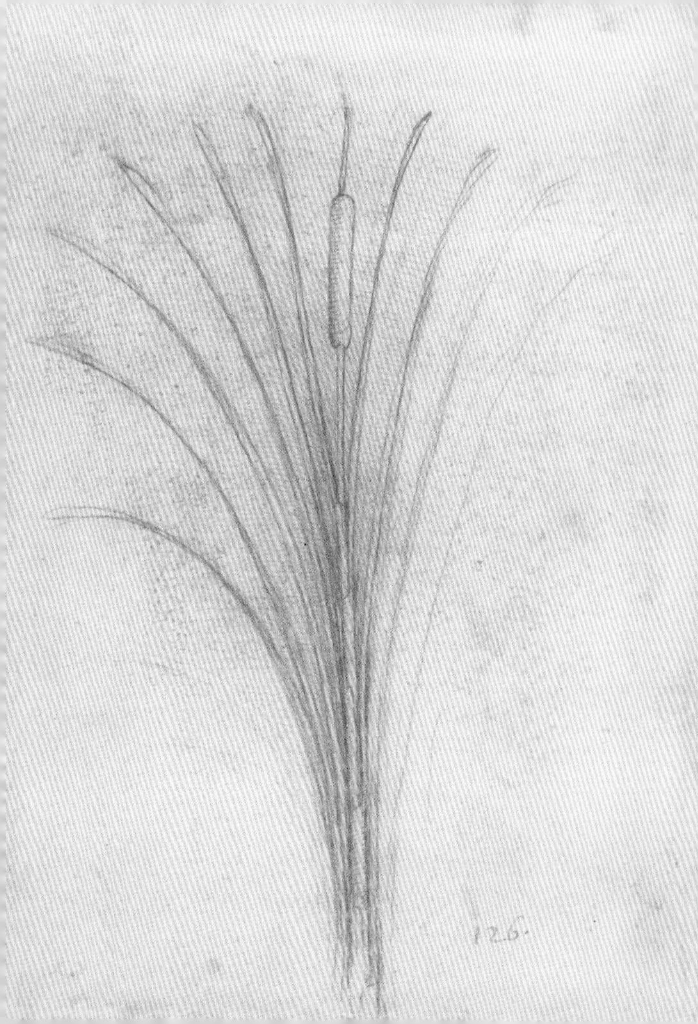
126.

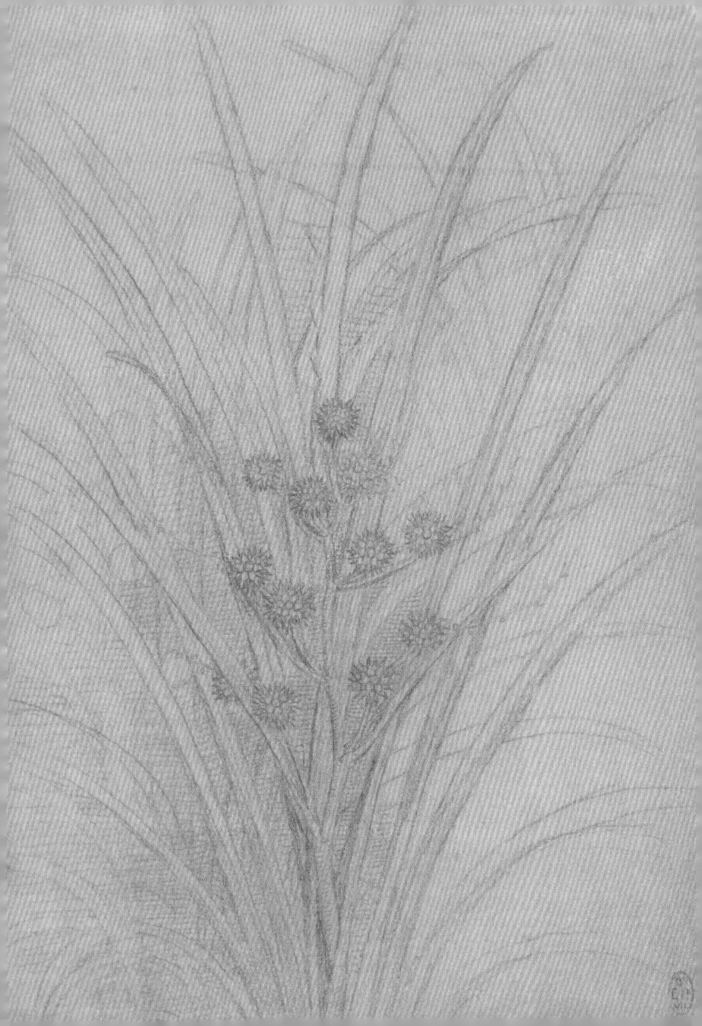

Finally, having grown old, he remained ill many months, and, feeling himself near to death, asked to have himself diligently informed of the teaching of the Catholic faith, and of the good way and holy Christian religion; and then, with many moans, he confessed and was penitent; and although he could not raise himself well on his feet, supporting himself on the arms of his friends and servants, he was pleased to take devoutly the most holy Sacrament from his bed. The King, who was wont often and lovingly to visit him, then came into the room; wherefore he, out of reverence, having raised himself to sit upon the bed, giving him an account of his sickness and the circumstances of it, showed withal how much he had offended God and mankind in not having worked at his art as he should have done. Thereupon he was seized by a paroxysm, the messenger of death; for which reason the King having risen and having taken his head, in order to assist him and show him favour, to the end that he might alleviate his pain, his spirit, which was divine, knowing that it could not have any greater honour, expired in the arms of the King, in the seventy-fifth year of his age.*

The loss of Leonardo grieved beyond measure all

* In fact Leonardo was 67 when he died.

those who had known him, since there was never anyone who did so much honour to painting. With the splendour of his aspect, which was very beautiful, he made serene every broken spirit: and with his words he turned to yea, or nay, every obdurate intention. By his physical force he could restrain any outburst of rage: and with his right hand he twisted the iron ring of a doorbell, or a horseshoe, as if it were lead. With his liberality he would assemble together and support his every friend, poor or rich, if only he had intellect and worth. He adorned and honoured, in every action, no matter what mean and bare dwelling; wherefore, in truth, Florence received a very great gift in the birth of Leonardo, and an incalculable loss in his death. In the art of painting, he added to the manner of colouring in oils a certain obscurity, whereby the moderns have given great force and relief to their figures. And in statuary, he proved his worth in the three figures of bronze that are over the door of San Giovanni, on the side towards the north, executed by Giovan Francesco Rustici, but contrived with the advice of Leonardo;[1] which are the most beautiful pieces of casting, the best designed, and the most perfect that

1. Preaching of St John the Baptist, 1506-11, still in situ at Baptistery, Florence; ill. opposite

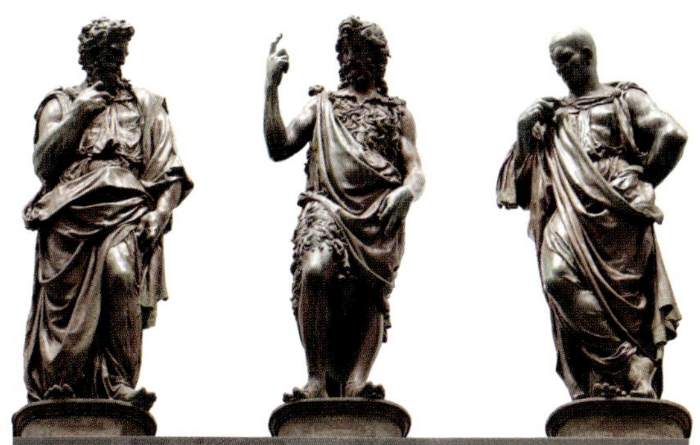

Giovan Francesco Rustici with advice from Leonardo, Preaching of St John the Baptist (with a Pharisee, left, and a Levite, right), 1506-11, Baptistery, Florence

have as yet been seen in modern days. By Leonardo we have the anatomy of the horse, and that of man even more complete. And so, on account of all his qualities, so many and so divine, although he worked much more by words than by deeds, his name and fame can never be extinguished; wherefore it was thus said in his praise by Messer Giovan Battista Strozzi:

> Vince costui pur solo
> Tutti altri; e vince Fidia e vince Apelle
> E tutto il lor vittorioso stuolo.*

* Alone this man vanquished all others; he vanquished Phidias, he vanquished Apelles, and all their victorious herd.

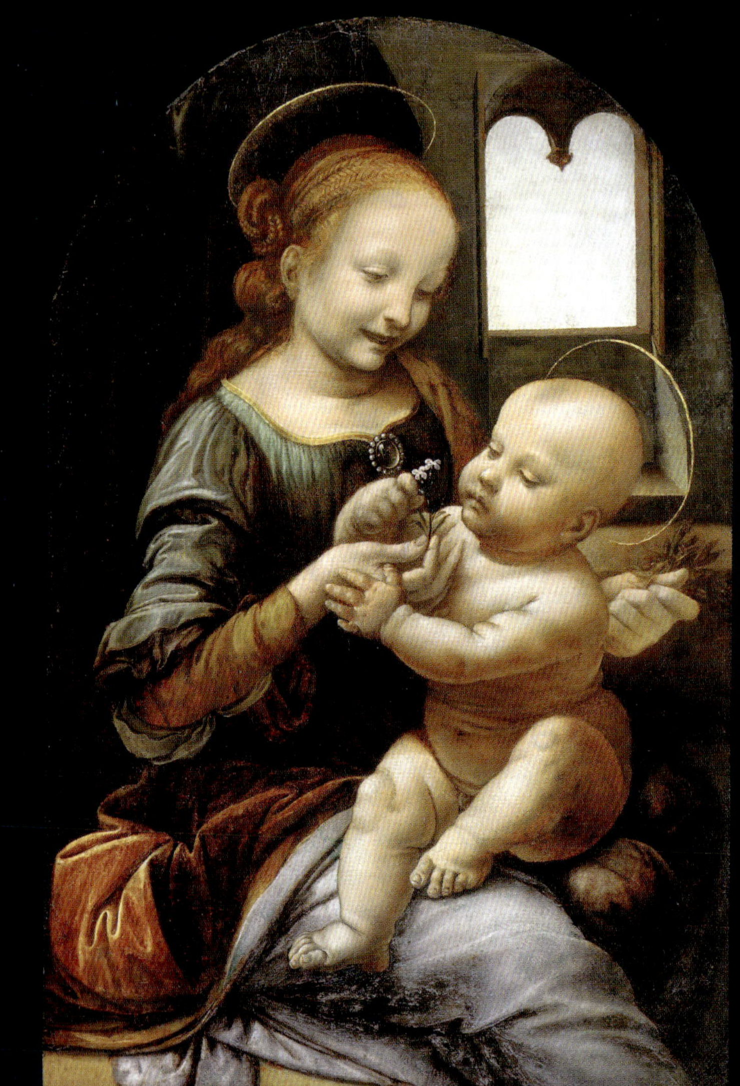

ANTONIO BILLI

Leonardo da Vinci, citizen of Florence

from his
commonplace book

c. 1522

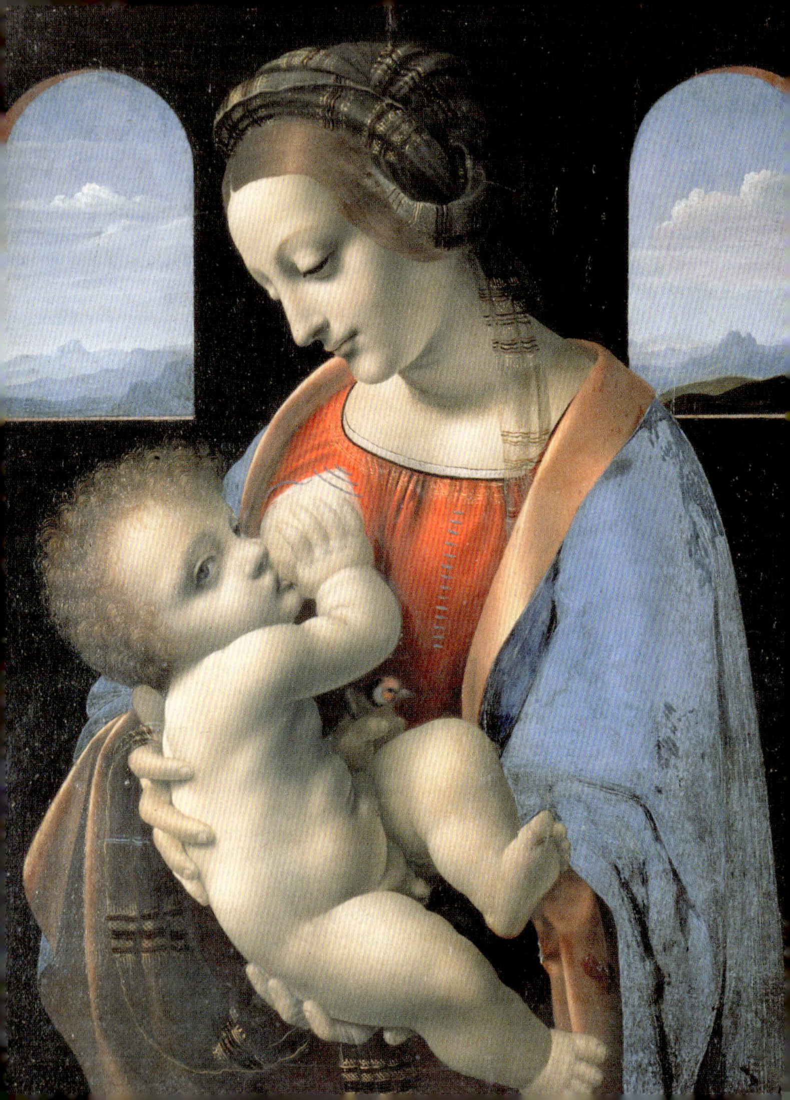

He was far in advance of others in design, and also in the most beautiful inventions, but he did not colour many things, because never and in nothing, not even the beautiful things he made did he satisfy himself; and for this reaons there are so very few things by him, his great knowledge of error prevented him from making them.

He made the portrait of Ginevra di Amerigho Benci, so beautifully finished that it seemed to be herself, no other.[1]

He made a Madonna on panel,[2] a very rare thing, and a St John.[3]

He made an altarpiece for Signor Lodovico of Milan, which has the reputation of being the most beautiful thing to be seen in painting, which the Signor sent to Germany to the Emperor.[4]

1. Washington, DC, National Gallery of Art, ill. p. 107 2. Unidentified, but three surviving candidates are the Madonna of the Carnation (ill. p. 49), the Madonna Benois (ill. p. 96) and the Madonna Litta (ill. opposite) 3. Unidentified. There is a St John in the Louvre, ill. p. 152 4. Possibly one of the two versions of the Virgin of the Rocks, see ill. p. 111

Opposite: Virgin and Child ('Madonna Litta'), c. 1490

P. 96: Virgin and Child ('Madonna Benois'), c. 1478

And in Milan he made a Last Supper, an excellent thing.[1]

He made in clay a horse of vast size, for the late duke Francesco Sforza, to cast in bronze; but that was judged impossible by everyone, because he wanted to cast it in one piece.[2]

He made an infinite number of marvellous drawings, amongst them a Madonna and St Anne, which went to France,[3] and a cartoon of the war of the Florentines, when they attacked Niccolo Piccinino, captain of the Duke of Milan, at Angshiari.[4] And this he began to transfer in the Council Chamber but the paint did not adhere, and so it remained unfinished. The fault lay with the fact that he was cheated over the linseed oil, which was adulterated.

He was universally talented in different things, such as drawing buildings and waters in perspective. And it is said, in drawing he surpassed all others until he drew his last breath; his ingenuity meant he was always making new things.

1. In situ, Santa Maria delle Grazie, Milan, ill. in fold-out pp. 58-60
2. Destroyed 3. Lost 4. Cartoon lost and painting destroyed

ANONIMO GADDIANO

Leonardo da Vinci

c. 1530

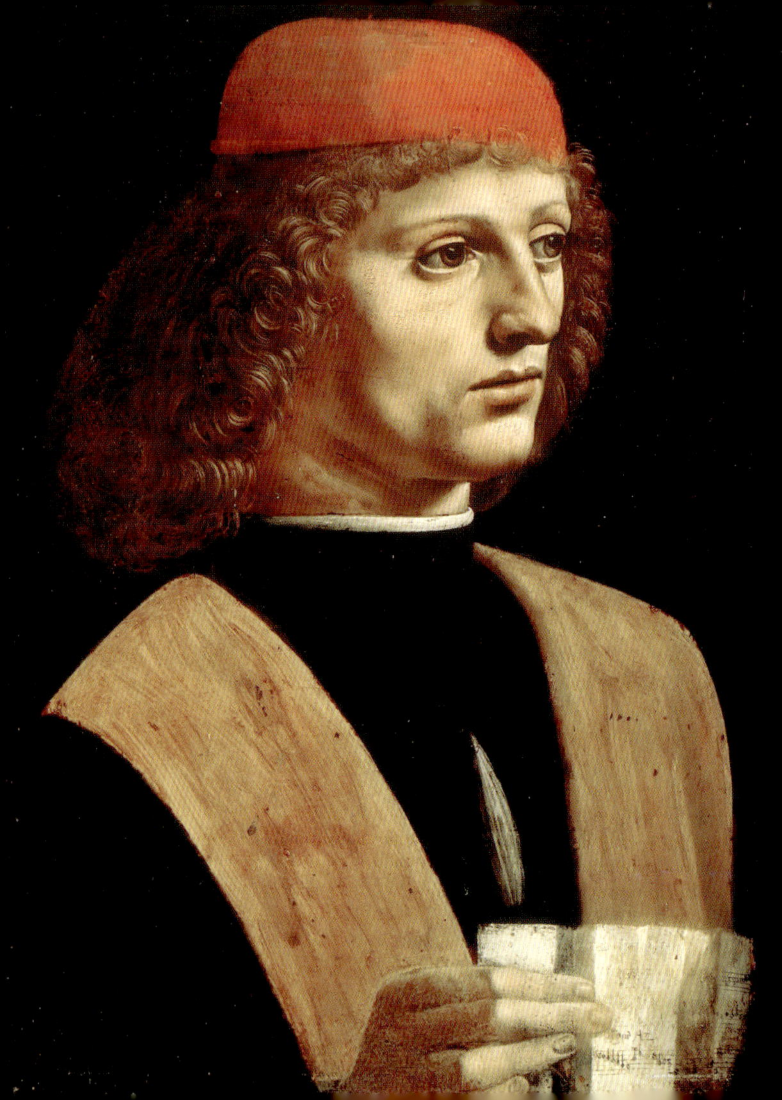

A Florentine citizen who, although he was the illegitimate son of Ser Piero da Vinci, was born of good blood on his mother's side. He was so unusual and many-sided that with him nature seemed to have produced a miracle, not only for the beauty of his person, but for the many gifts with which she endowed him and which he fully mastered. Greatly talented in mathematics, he was no less so in the science of perspective, while in the field of sculpture and design he far surpassed all others. He made many excellent inventions, but because it was hard for him to be satisfied with his work we find but few paintings from his hand. An eloquent speaker, he was an exquisite musician on the *lira* and taught the singer Atalante Migliorotti. He was delightfully inventive, and was most skillful in lifting weights, in building waterworks and other imaginative constructions, nor did his mind ever come to rest, but dwelt always with ingenuity on the creation of new inventions.

As a young man he was with Lorenzo de' Medici the Magnificent, and with his support he worked in the gardens of his palace in San Marco in Florence.

Opposite: Portrait of a Musician, c. 1485. The sitter has sometimes been identified as Atalante Migliorotti

When he was thirty years of age it is said that the Magnificent sent him to the Duke of Milan to present, with Atalante Migliorotti, the gift of a *lira*, which the latter could play with rare execution. Later he returned to Florence where he remained for some time, but then, either because of some kind of indignation or other causes, while working in the hall of the Council of the Signoria, he left and went back to Milan where he served the Duke for a few years. Afterwards he was with Cesare Borgia, the Duke of Valentinois, and then also in France in several places, before returning to Milan. While preparing to cast his equestrian monument in bronze[1] a revolution in the state brought him back to Florence, where for six months he stayed in the house of Giovanni Francesco Rustici, sculptor of the via Martelli. Once more he returned to Milan, and then finally went to France in the service of the king, Francis I. He took with him enough of his drawings, leaving some again in the Hospital of Santa Maria Nuova, Florence, together with other household goods, and the greater part of

1. Commissioned in 1482, but never completed

Opposite: Portrait of a Woman ('La Belle Ferronière'), c. 1493-94. Sometimes said to be Lucrezia Crivelli, mistress of Lodovico Sforza

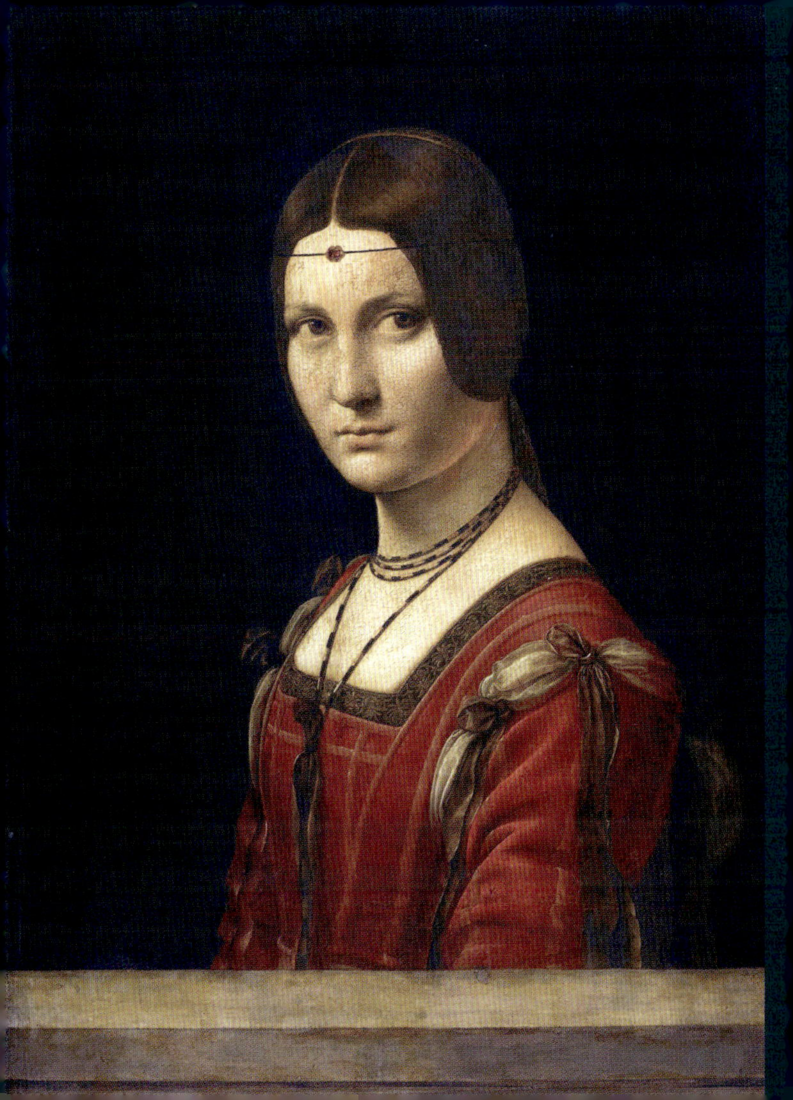

a cartoon in the Council Hall, of which the design of a group of horses can be seen today in the Palace.[1] He died near Amboise, a French city, at the age of seventy-two [in fact sixty-seven], in a place called Cloux, which he had made his home. In his will he left everything to Messer Francesco da Melzi, a nobleman of Milan, all his money and clothes, books, writings, drawings, instruments, and his treatises on painting, art and his industriousness, and whatever else could be found, and made him executor of his will. To his servant Battista Villani he left half of his garden on the outskirts of Milan, and the other half to Salai, his pupil. He left four hundred ducats to his brothers, depositing the sum in the Hospital of Santa Maria Nuova in Florence, but after his death only three hundred ducats were found.

Among his pupils were Salai of Milan, Zoroastro of Peretola, Riccio Fiorentino of the Porta della Croce, Ferrando the Spaniard, who worked with him in the Hall of the Signoria Palace.

In Florence he painted the portrait of Ginevra d'Amerigho Benci from nature,[2] a work which was

1. The cartoon is lost; the painting was covered over in 1563
2. 1474-78, Washington, DC, National Gallery of Art, ill. opposite

Opposite: Portrait of Ginevra de' Benci, c. 1474-78

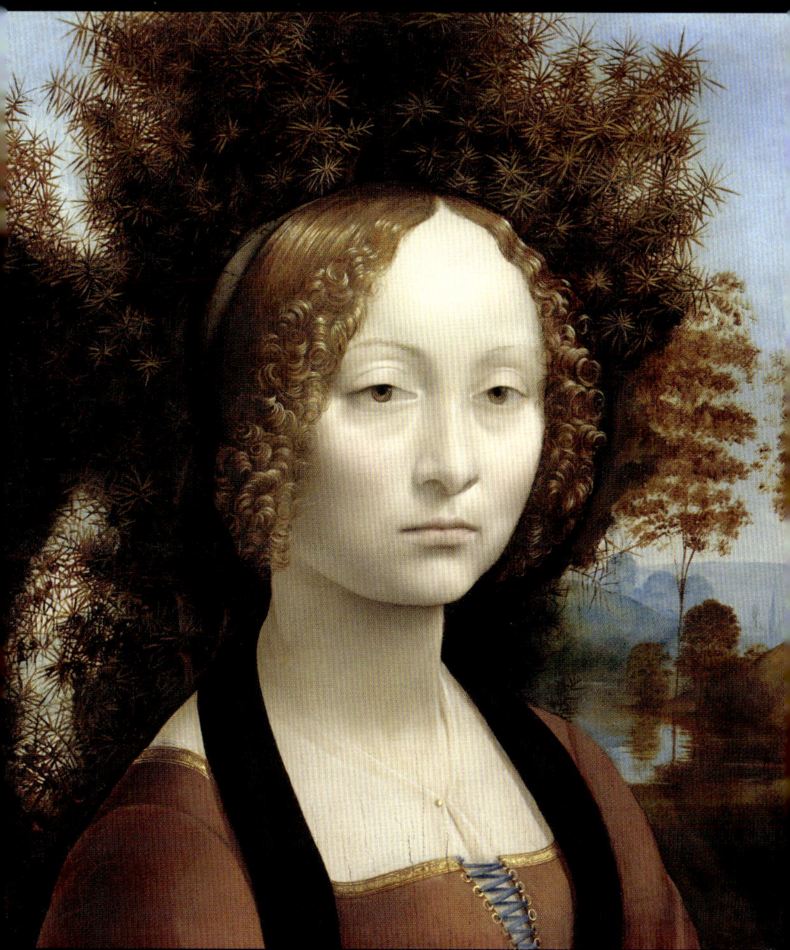

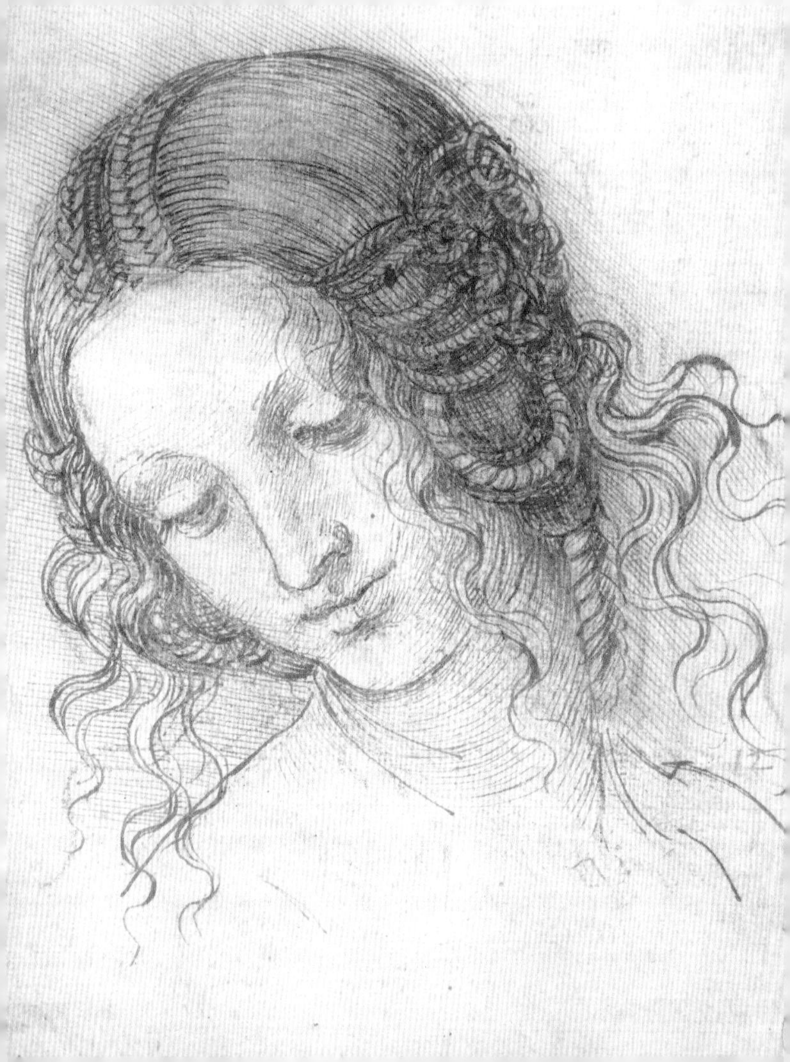

so finished that it seemed not a portrait but Ginevra herself.

He made a panel of Our Lady, a most excellent work.[1] He also painted a St John.[2]

And again a Leda.[3] He painted Adam and Eve in watercolour, today in the house of Messer Ottaviano de' Medici.[4]

He made the portrait from nature of Piero Francesco del Giocondo.[5]

He painted … a head of Medusa with a wonderful and unique collection of serpents; today it is in the chamber of the most Illustrious and Excellent Signor Duke Cosimo de' Medici.[6]

He was commissioned to paint in the great Council Hall of the Palace in Florence a cartoon of the battle of Florentines, during the time at Anghiari when they attacked Niccholo Piccin[in]o, the captain of Duke Filippo of Milan, and he began work in that place as can be seen there today; and with varnish.[7]

He undertook to paint a panel in the same Palace,

1. Unidentified 2. A painting of St John survives in the Louvre, ill. p. 152 3. Lost but preparatory drawings survive (see ill. opposite), as do copies by pupils. 4. Lost 5. Lost, or possibly confused with the painting of Mona Lisa, wife of Piero Francesco del Giocondo, ill. p. 78 6. Lost 7. 1503-6, covered up by Vasari in 1563

Opposite: Study for the head of Leda, c. 1504-6

which was later finished after his design by Filippo di Fra Filippo.[1]

He painted an altar panel for Signor (the Duke) Lodovico of Milan, which those who have seen it declare to be the most beautiful and unusual work to be found in painting, and which the aforementioned lord sent to the Emperor.[2]

He also painted in Milan a Last Supper, a most excellent work.[3]

Again in Milan he likewise made a horse of immense grandeur, bearing upon it the Duke Francesco Sforza, a most beautiful work which was to be cast in bronze, a feat universally judged impossible, especially since he said he desired to cast it all in one piece; this work was never realized.[4]

He made innumerable drawings, all marvellous things, and among them a Madonna and St Anne,[5] which went to France, and anatomical studies which he drew in the Hospital of Santa Maria Nuova in Florence.[6]

1. Filippino Lippi, Virgin and Four Saints, 1485, Uffizi, Florence 2. Unidentified, but possibly one of the versions of the Madonna of the Rocks (National Gallery, London, ill. opposite; Louvre, Paris) 3. Still in situ, Santa Maria della Grazie, Milan 4. Clay model destroyed 5. Lost 6. Numerous anatomical drawings survive

Opposite: The Madonna of the Rocks (London version), c. 1495–1508

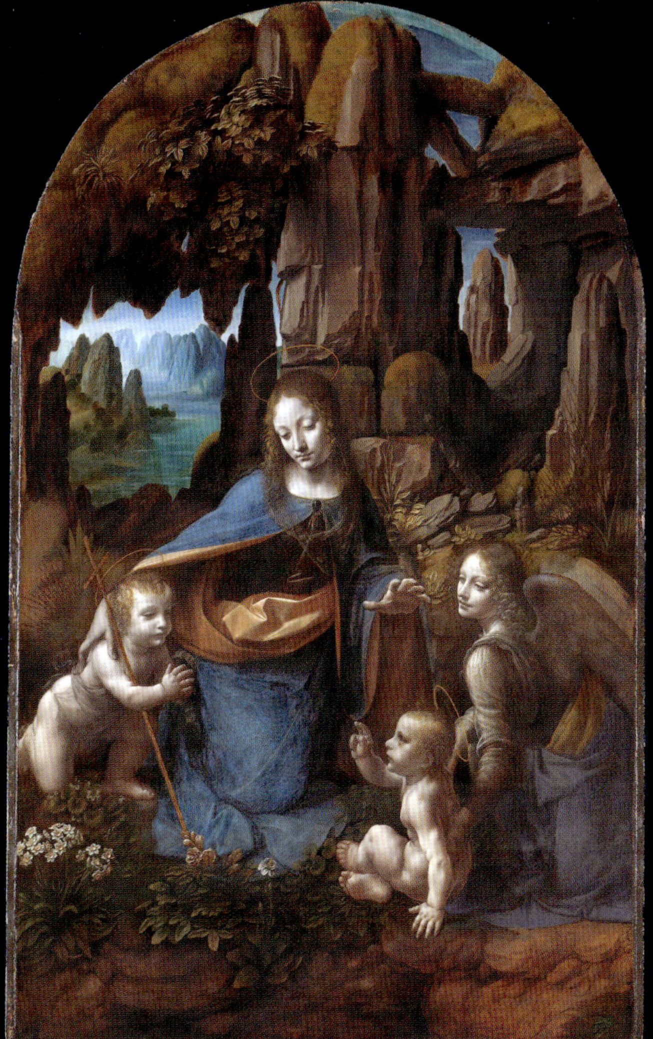

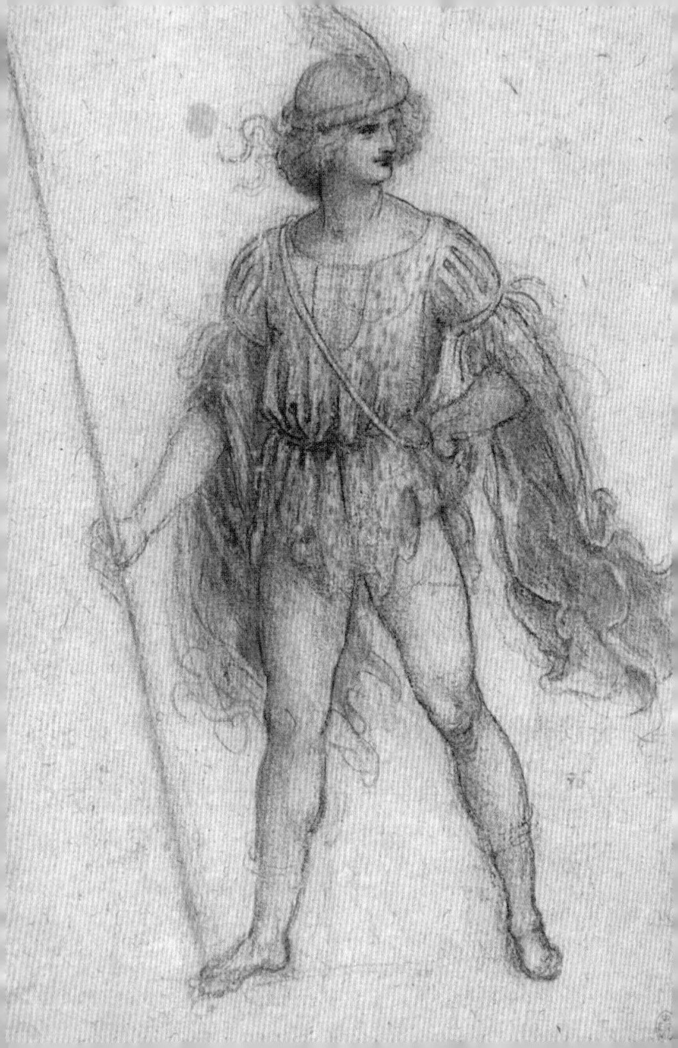

*From [Giovanni da] Gav[ina]**

Leonardo da Vinci was a contemporary of Michelangelo, and from Pliny he took the recipe for the pigments with which he painted, but without fully understanding it. The first time he demonstrated it upon a wall in the Hall of the Pope, where he was working, he placed a great fire of burning coals in front of it, whereby through the heat the material would be dried and fixed. After that, desiring to put the work in the Hall (of the Council), it turned out that the fire dried and joined the lower part of the fresco, but was unable to reach the upper section, due to the great distance, and this part did not come together and the colours ran.

Beautiful in person and aspect, Leonardo was well-proportioned and graceful. He wore a rose-coloured cloak, which came only to his knees although at the time long vestments were the custom. His beard came

*The following lines are headed 'Dal Gav' or 'Cav' in the manuscript, which appears to indicate that they were supplied to the Anonimo either by the painter Giovannia da Gavina, or possibly by the sculptor Baccio Bandinelli, who was a papal knight (Cavaliere)

Opposite: Masquerader as a lansquenet, c. 1517-18

to the middle of his breast and was well-dressed and curled.

Leonardo, in the company of Giovanni da Gavina of Santa Trinità, passed the benches of the Palazzo Spini one day, where a group of gentlemen were arguing over a passage in Dante. They appealed to Leonardo to explain the lines to them. Exactly at this moment Michelangelo passed by and Leonardo replied to the questioners, 'Michelangelo will explain it to you'. Michelangelo responded with anger, since it seemed to him that Leonardo was making mock of him, 'You made a design for a horse to be cast in bronze, and, unable to cast it, have in your shame abandoned it'. And saying this, he turned his back to them and went his way. And Leonardo stood there, and turned red at these words.

And to annoy Leonardo, Michelangelo called after him: 'And those Milanese idiots did believe in you!'

PAOLO GIOVIO
BISHOP OF NOCERA

The Life of Leonardo da Vinci

from
Notable men and women of our time

c. 1528

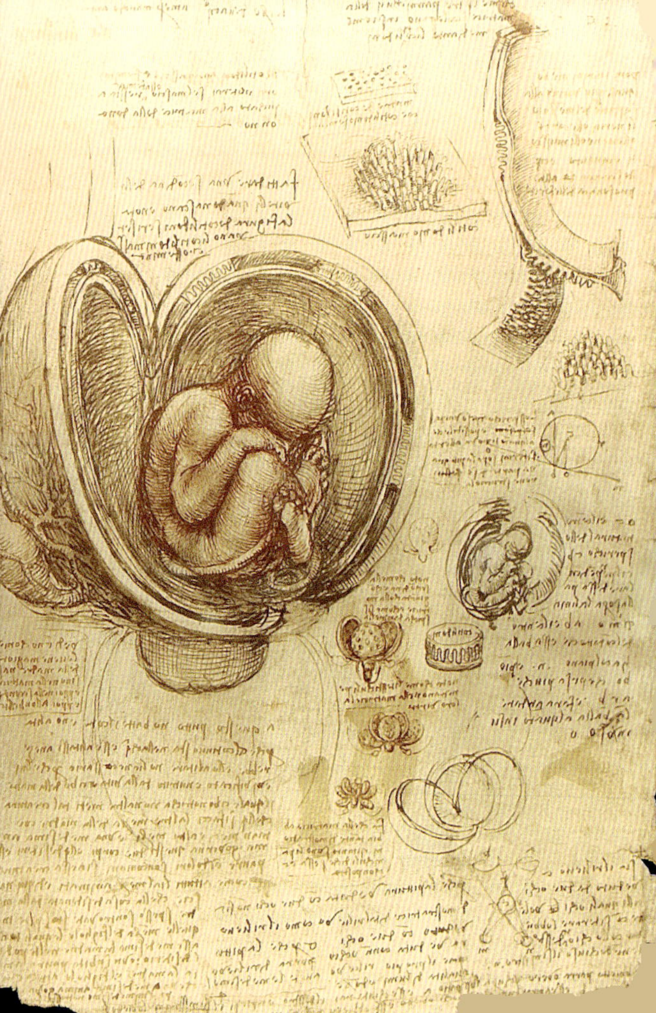

Leonardo, born at Vinci, an insignificant hamlet in Tuscany, has added great lustre to the art of painting. He established that all proper practice of this art should be preceded by a training in the sciences and the liberal arts which he regarded as the necessary handmaidens to painting. He placed modelling as a means of rendering figures in relief on a flat surface before other processes done with the brush. The science of optics was to him of paramount importance and on it he founded the principles of the distribution of light and shade down to the most minute details. In order that he might be able to paint the various joints and muscles as they bend and stretch according to the laws of nature, he dissected in medical schools the corpses of criminals, indifferent to this inhuman and nauseating work. He then tabulated with extreme accuracy all the different parts down to the smallest veins and the composition of the bones, in order that this work on which he had spent so many years should be published from copper engravings for the benefit of art. But while he was thus spending his time in the close research of subordinate branches of his art he carried only very few works to completion; for owing to his

Opposite: The foetus in the womb, c. 1511

masterly facility and fastidiousness of his nature, he discarded works he had already begun. However, the wall painting at Milan of Christ at Supper with His Disciples is greatly admired.[1] It is said that when King Louis saw it he coveted it so much that he inquired anxiously from those standing around him whether it could be detached from the wall and transported forthwith to France, although this would have destroyed the famous refectory. There is also the picture of the infant Christ playing with His mother, the Virgin, and His grandmother, Anne, which King Francis of France bought and placed in his chapel.[2] Moreover, there remains the painting of the battle and victory over the Pisans in the Council Chamber at Florence which was extraordinarily magnificent but came to an untimely end owing to the defective plaster which persistently rejected the colours ground in walnut oil.[3] It seems as if the very natural regret caused by this unexpected injury and interruption of the work was instrumental in making it famous. For Lodovico Sforza he made also a clay model of a colossal horse

1. Still in situ, Milan, Santa Maria delle Grazie, ill. in foldout pp. 58-60 2. 1503-19, Paris, Louvre, ill. opposite 3. 1503-6, covered up by Vasari in 1563

Opposite: Virgin and Child with St Anne, c. 1503-19

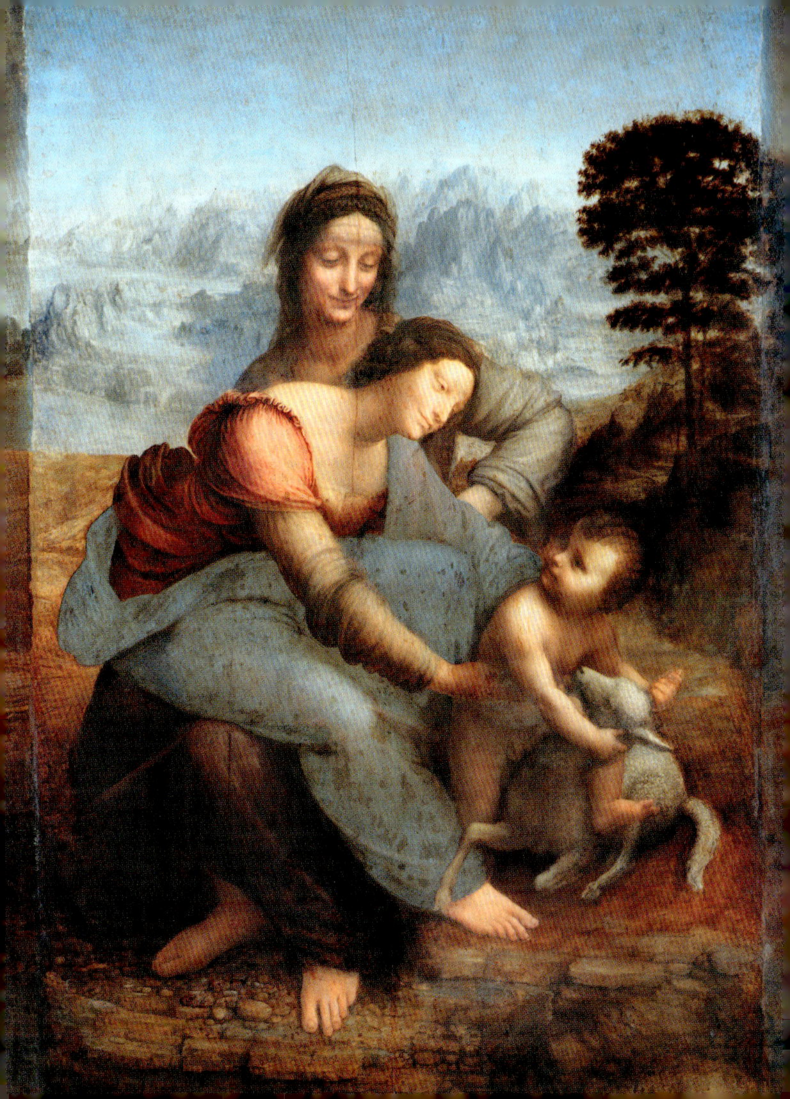

to be cast in bronze, on which was to be seated the figure of the famous condottiere Francesco, Lodovico's father.[1] The vehement lifelike action of this horse as if panting is amazing, not less so the sculptor's skill and his consummate knowledge of nature. His charm of disposition, his brilliancy and generosity were not less than the beauty of his appearance. His genius for invention was astounding, and he was the arbiter of all questions relating to beauty and elegance, especially in pageantry. He sang beautifully to his own accompaniment on the *lira* to the delight of the entire court. He died in France at the age of sixty-seven to the grief of his friends, which loss was all the greater for among the great crowd of young men who contributed to the success of his studio he left no disciple of outstanding fame.

1. Clay model destroyed

MATTEO BANDELLO

Concerning the 'Last Supper'

from

The Novels: Introduction to the Fiftieth Story

1540

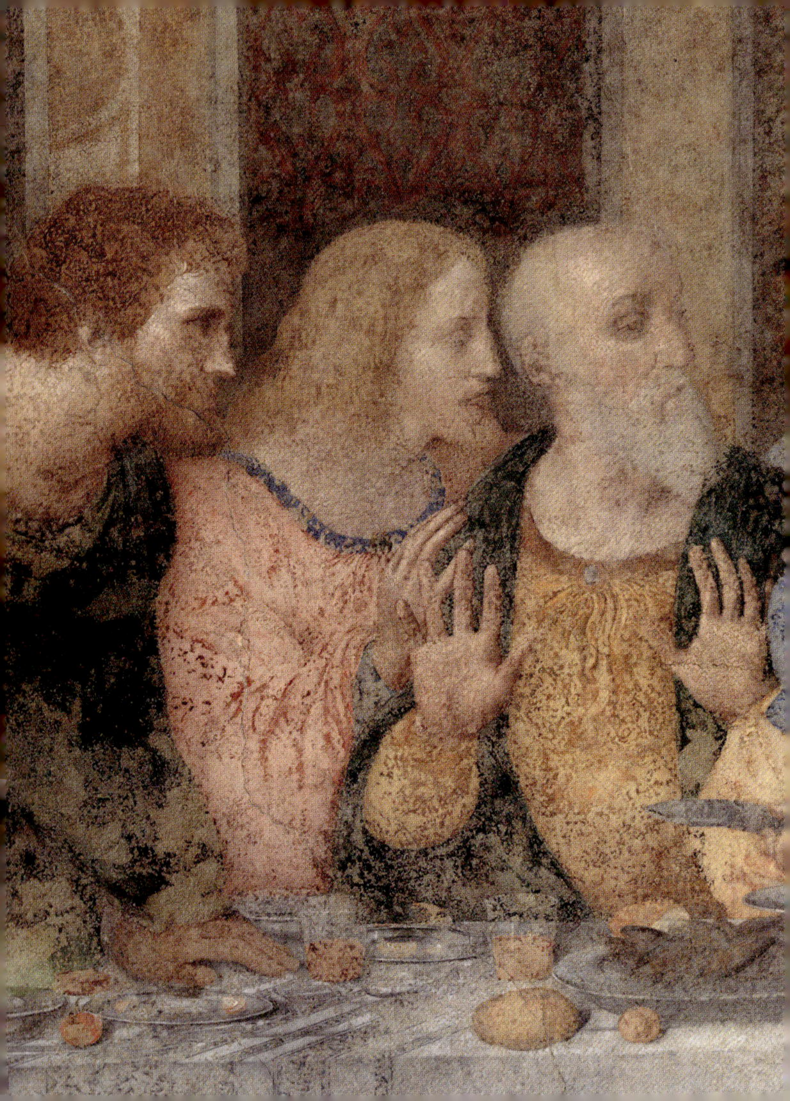

In Lodovico's time, some gentlemen living in Milan used to meet in the monks' refectory of the convent delle Grazie, where with hushed voices they watched the excellent painter Leonardo da Vinci of Florence as he was finishing his marvellous and most famous picture of the Last Supper.[1] The painter was well pleased that each should tell him what they thought of his work. Now the said Leonardo would often come to the convent at early dawn (and this I have seen him do myself), hastily mount the scaffolding — for the Last Supper is high above the ground — and work from sunrise until the shades of evening compelled him to cease, without once laying his brush aside, nor thinking to take food or drink at all. At other times he would remain there three or four days without touching his picture, only coming for a few hours to remain before it, gazing at his figures as if to criticize them himself. At midday, too, when the glare of a sun at its zenith has emptied all the streets of Milan, I have seen him, as the whim took him, hasten from the citadel, where he was modelling

1. Still in situ, Milan, Santa Maria delle Grazie, ill. in fold-out, pp. 58-60

Opposite: Detail from the Last Supper, 1495-98. The central figure, St James the Less, has been suggested as a self-portrait

his colossal horse, without seeking the shade, by the shortest way to the convent, where he would climb the scaffolding, take his brush to add a touch or two to one of his figures, and then as suddenly come down and leave.

At the time Cardinal Gurcense the Elder was living at the monastery and happened to come into the refectory, to see the Last Supper, at a time when the gentlemen I have mentioned were also there. When Leonardo saw the prelate, he came down to do him reverence, and was graciously received and made much of. Then the conversation ranged widely, but especially about the excellency of the art of painting, some of the company wishing that it might be possible to see the paintings of antiquity so praised by worthy writers, so that they could judge if the painters of our time have equalled the ancients. The cardinal asked what salary the painter had of the duke, and Leonardo replied that he had two thousand ducats of regular pension, without reckoning the gifts and presents whith the duke most liberally made him all day long. This seemed a great amount to the cardinal, who presently left the refectory and returned to his quarters...

SABBA DA CASTIGLIONE

Concerning Leonardo

from

Ricordi ovvero ammaestramenti

1554

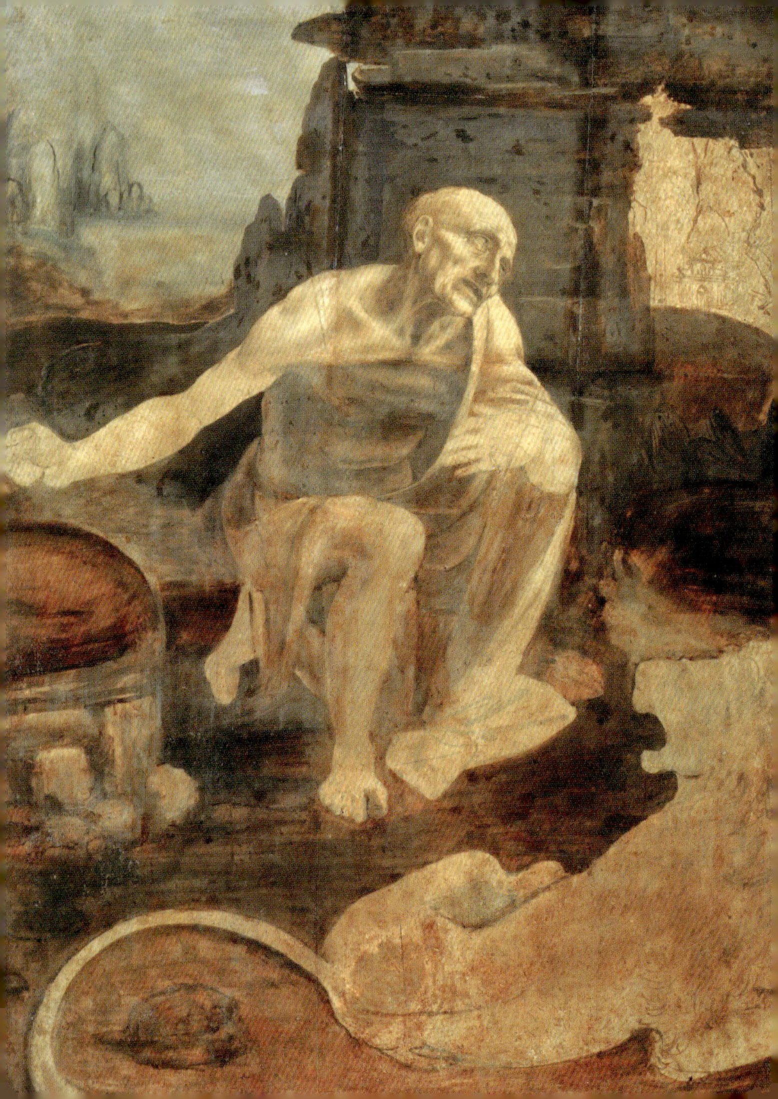

There's Leonardo da Vinci, a man of great inventiveness, very excellent in painting and the most famous disciple of Verrocchio, known for the sweetness of his manner, and the first inventor of large figures defined by the manipulation of shadow and lighting, as seen in the refectory of Santa Maria delle Grazie in Milan (certainly a divine work, known throughout the whole world as famous and celebrated). There are few other works by his hand to be found, because when he should have dedicated himself to painting, in which without doubt he would have proved to be a new Apelles, he gave himself over completely geometry, to architecture and anatomy, and furthermore he worked on modelling the horse of Milan, taking a full sixteen years, and certainly the worth of this work was such that one could not say that he had wasted time and effort, but through ignorance and negligence of some (who having no understanding of the virtues think them worthless) it was left to be destroyed disgracefully, and I remember (it pains and displeases me to say) that such a noble and inspired work was used for target practise by Gascon crossbowmen.

Opposite: St Jerome, c. 1480. This unfinished painting illustrates Leonardo's interest in anatomy and 'the manipulation of shadow and lighting' at this period

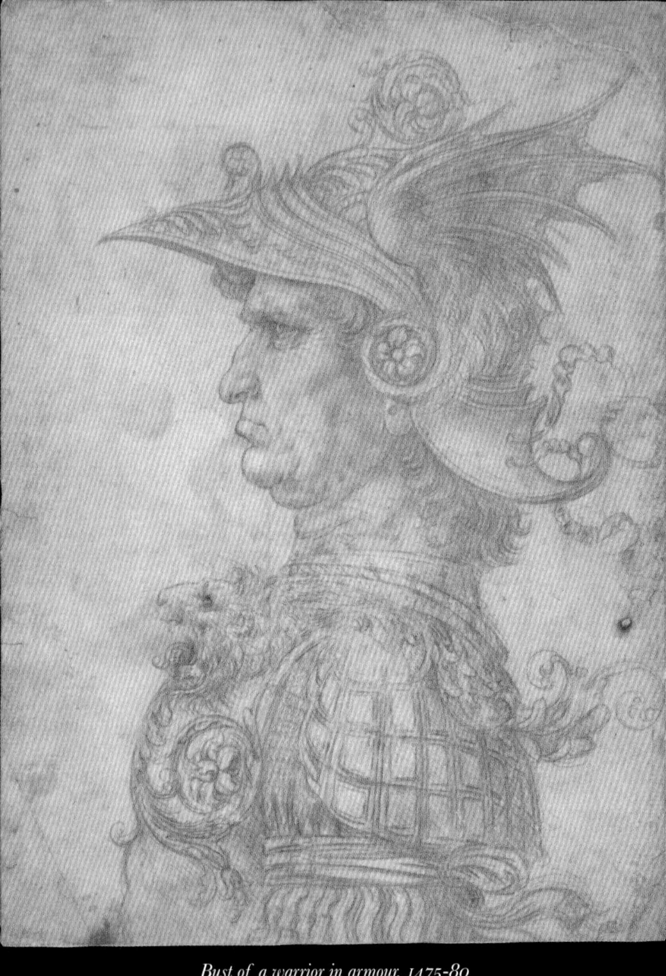

Bust of a warrior in armour, 1475-80

LEONARDO DA VINCI

Draft of a letter to Lodovico Sforza, in which Leonardo offers his services and states his abilities

c. 1482

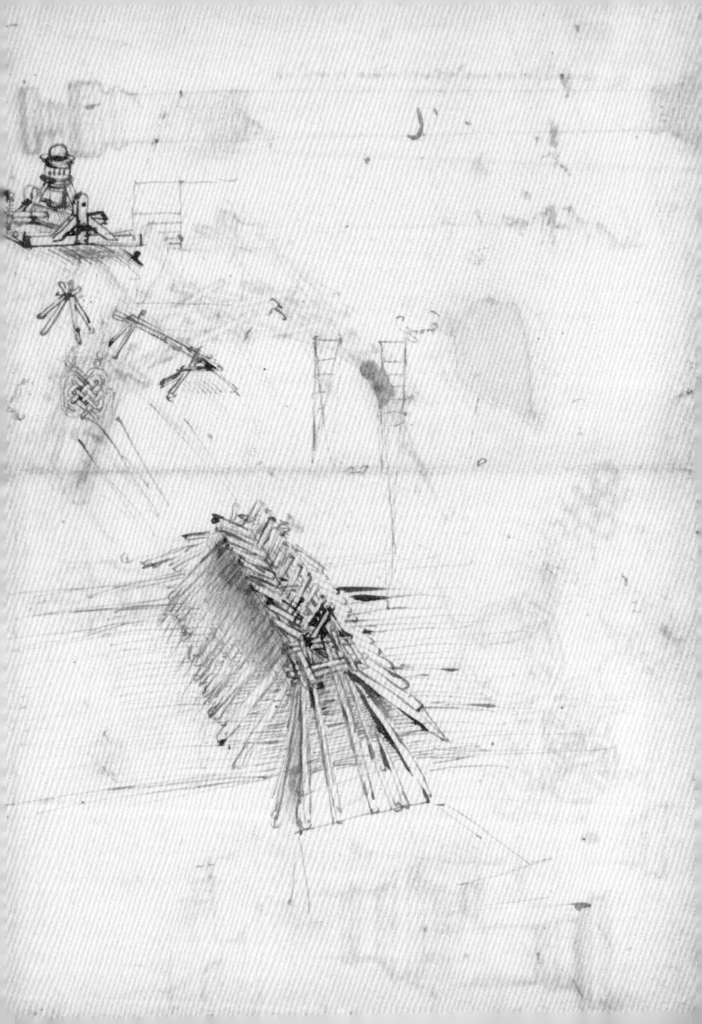

Most Illustrious Lord, Having now sufficiently considered the specimens of all those who proclaim themselves skilled contrivers of instruments of war, and that the invention and operation of the said instruments are nothing different from those in common use, I shall endeavour, without prejudice to anyone else, to explain myself to your Excellency, showing your Lordship my secrets, and then offering them to your best pleasure and approbation to work with effect at opportune moments on all those things which, in part, shall be briefly noted below.

{1} I have a sort of extremely light and strong bridges, adapted to be most easily carried, and with them you may pursue, and at any time flee from the enemy; and others, secure and indestructible by fire and battle, easy and convenient to lift and place. Also methods of burning and destroying those of the enemy.

{2} I know how, when a place is besieged, to take the water out of the trenches, and make endless variety of bridges and covered ways and ladders, and other machines pertaining to such expeditions.

{3} Item. If, by reason of the height of the banks,

Opposite: Design for a portable bridge, c. 1485

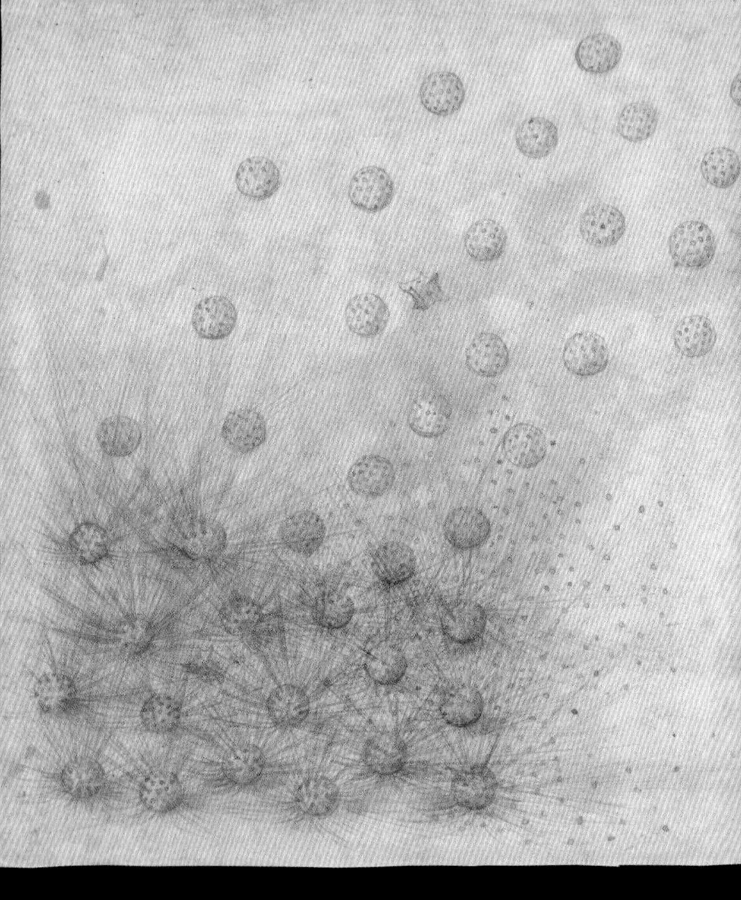

Mortar bombardment with explosive shells, c. 1485

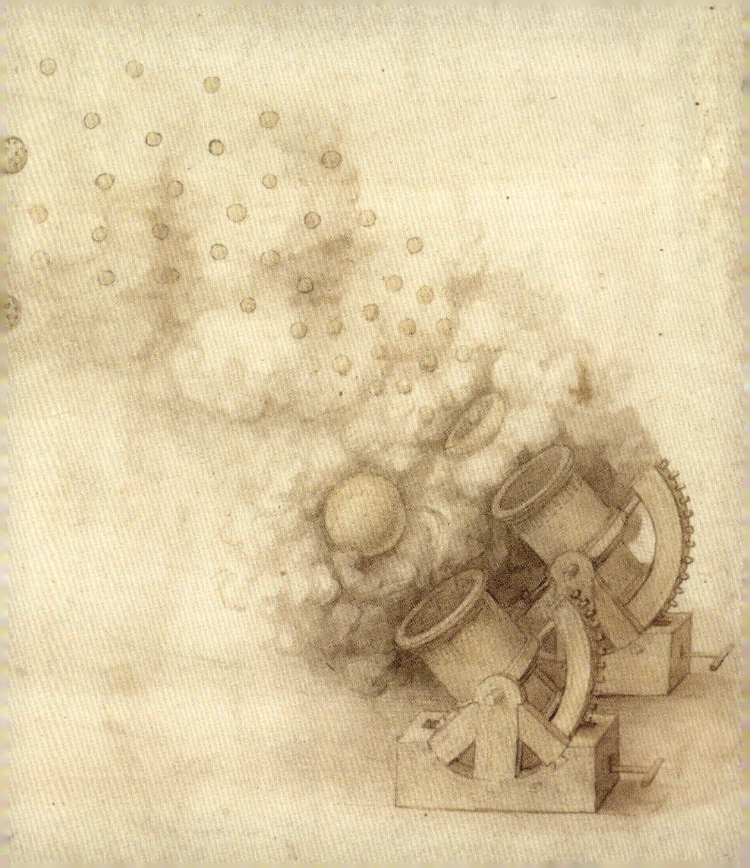

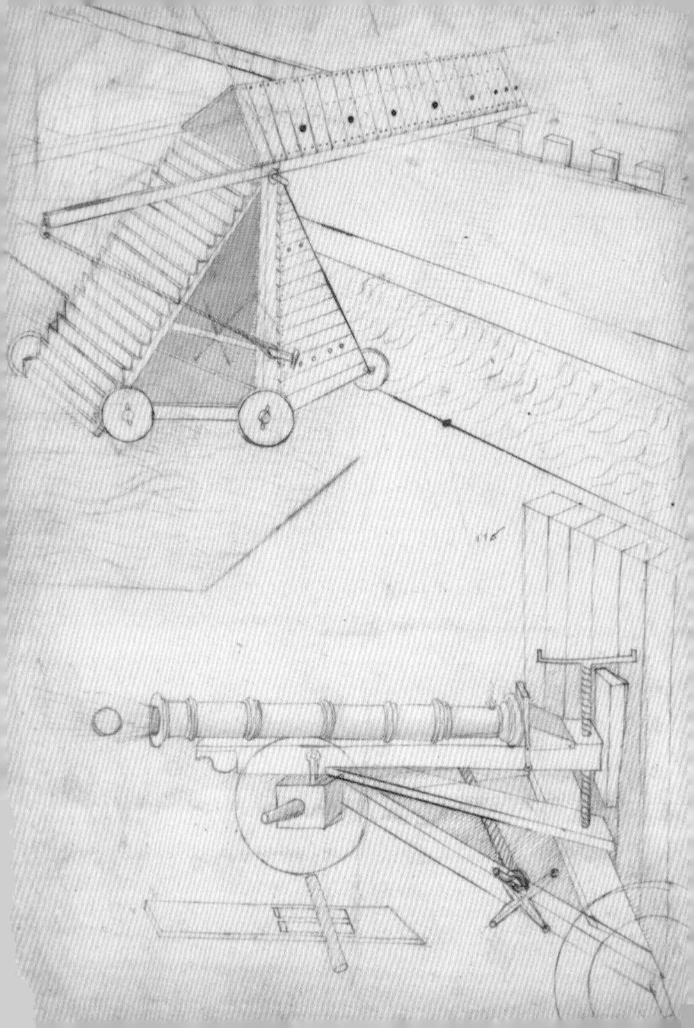
116

or the strength of the place, and its position, it is impossible, when besieging a place, to avail oneself of the plan of bombardment, I have methods for destroying every rock or other fortress, even if it were founded on a rock, &c.

{4} Again, I have kinds of mortars, most convenient and easy to carry; and with these I can fling small stones almost resembling a storm; and with the smoke of these cause great terror to the enemy, to his great detriment and confusion.

{5} Item. I have means by secret and tortuous mines and ways, made without noise, to reach a designated [spot], even if it were needed to pass under a trench or a river.

{6} Item. I will make covered chariots, safe and unassailable, which, entering among the enemy with their artillery, there is no body of men so great but they would break them. And behind these, infantry could follow quite unhurt and without hindrance.

{7} Item. In case of need I will make big guns, mortars, and light ordnance of fine and useful forms, out of the common type.

{8} Where the operation of bombardment might

Opposite: Siege machinery, c. 1479-80

Overleaf: Military machines, c. 1485

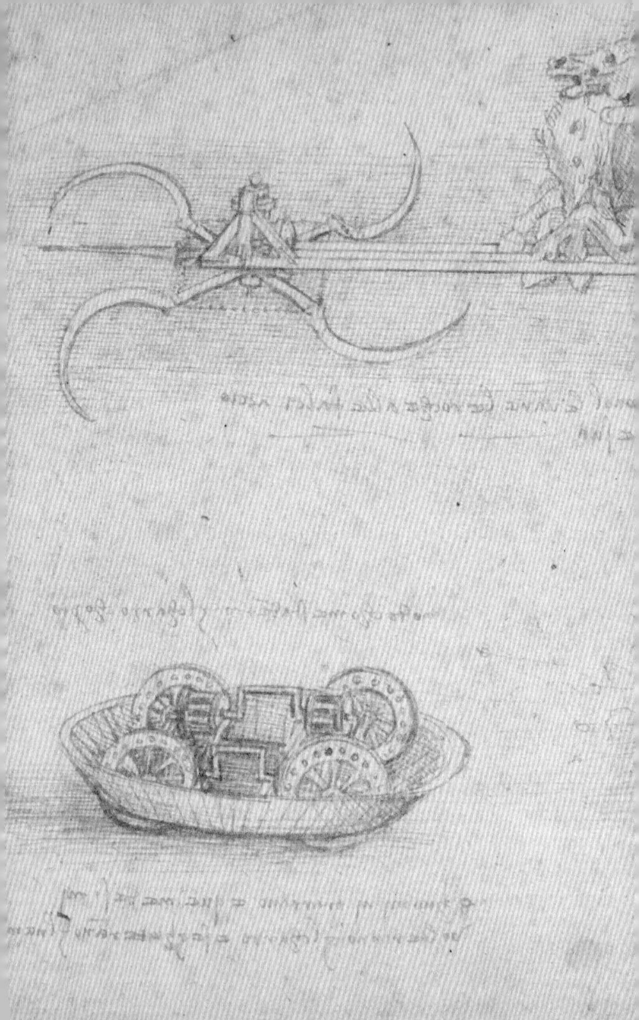

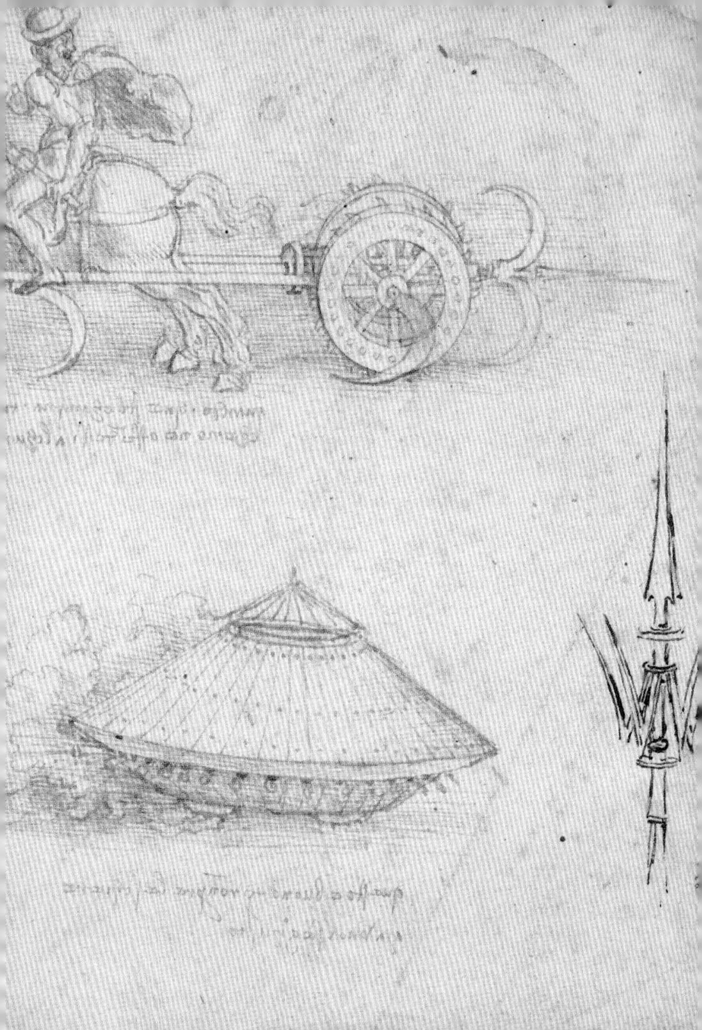

fail, I would contrive catapults, mangonels, *trabocchi*, and other machines of marvellous efficacy and not in common use. And in short, according to the variety of cases, I can contrive various and endless means of offence and defence.

{9} And if the fight should be at sea I have many kinds of machines most efficient for offence and defence; and vessels which will resist the attack of the largest guns and powder and fumes.

{10} In time of peace I believe I can give perfect satisfaction and to the equal of any other in architecture and the composition of buildings public and private; and in guiding water from one place to another.

Item. I can carry out sculpture in marble, bronze, or clay, and also I can do in painting whatever may be done, as well as any other, be he who he may.

Again, the bronze horse may be taken in hand, which is to be to the immortal glory and eternal honour of the prince your father of happy memory, and of the illustrious house of Sforza.

And if any of the above-named things seem to any one to be impossible or not feasible, I am most ready to make the experiment in your park, or in whatever place may please your Excellency – to whom I commend myself with the utmost humility, &c.

FRA PIETRO DA NOVELLARA

Correspondence with Isabella d'Este, Marchioness of Mantua

1501

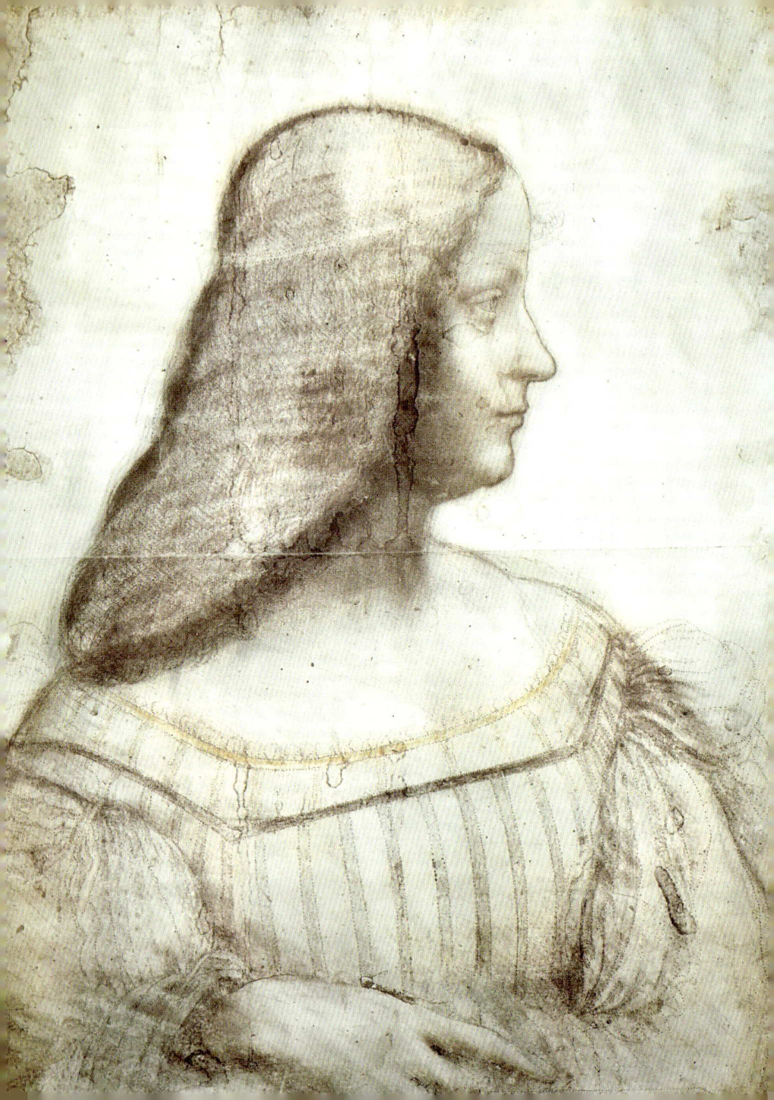

MANTUA, 27 MARCH 1501

Isabella to Fra Pietro da Novellara asking for a Madonna and a portrait from Leonardo da Vinci

If Leonardo Fiorentino the painter is to be found there in Florence, we beg you to discover what his situation is, and whether he has got underway with any work, as I hear that he has, and what work it is, and if you think he is likely to be staying there for some time. Thus Your Reverence could sound him out, as you know how, as to whether he intends to take up the commission to paint a picture for our study: if he is willing to do it, we will leave to his judgement both the theme of the picture and the date of delivery. And if you find him reluctant, you could at least try to persuade him to do me a little picture of the Madonna, in that devout and sweet style which is his natural gift. Would you also ask him to be so good as to send me another sketch of his portrait of us, since His Lordship our consort has given away the one he left here. If all this is done I will be very grateful to you, and to Leonardo himself for what he offers me…

Opposite: Portrait drawing of Isabella d'Este, 1499-1500

FLORENCE, 3 APRIL 1501

Fra Pietro da Novellara to Isabella d'Este about the St Anne cartoon

Most illustrious and excellent Lady,

I have just received Your Ladyship's letter, and will attend to your requests with all speed and diligence, but from what I understand Leonardo's life is extremely irregular and haphazard, and he seems to live from day to day. Since he has been in Florence he has only done one drawing, in a cartoon. It shows an infant Christ, of about one year old, almost escaping from the arms of his mother. He has got hold of a lamb and seems to be squeezing it. The mother, almost raising herself from the lap of St Anne, holds on to the child in order to draw him away from the lamb, which signifies the Passion. St Anne is rising somewhat from her seat; it seems that she wants to restrain her daughter from trying to separate the child from the lamb, which perhaps symbolizes the Church's desire that the Passion should not be impeded from running its course. These figures are life-size, but the cartoon is not so large because they are all seated or leaning over, and each figure is partly in front of another, towards

1. Lost, but see ill. of painting of same subject, p. 119

the left-hand side. This drawing is not yet finished. He has not done anything else, though two of his assistants make copies, and he from time to time adds some touches to them. He devotes much of his time to geometry, and has no fondness at all for the paintbrush. I am writing this only so Your Ladyship should know that I have received your letter. I will do what you ask and advise Your Ladyship as soon as possible.

FLORENCE, 14 APRIL 1501

Fra Pietro da Novellara to Isabella d'Este about the Madonna of the Yarnwinder

Most illustrious and excellent Lady,

During this Holy Week I have learned of the intentions of Leonardo the painter, by means of his pupil Salai and some others who are close to him, and to make his intentions clear they brought him to me on Holy Wednesday [7 April]. In short, his mathematical experiments have distracted him so much from painting that he cannot abide the paintbrush. I apprised him of Your Ladyship's wishes and found him very willing to satisfy them, for the kindness you showed

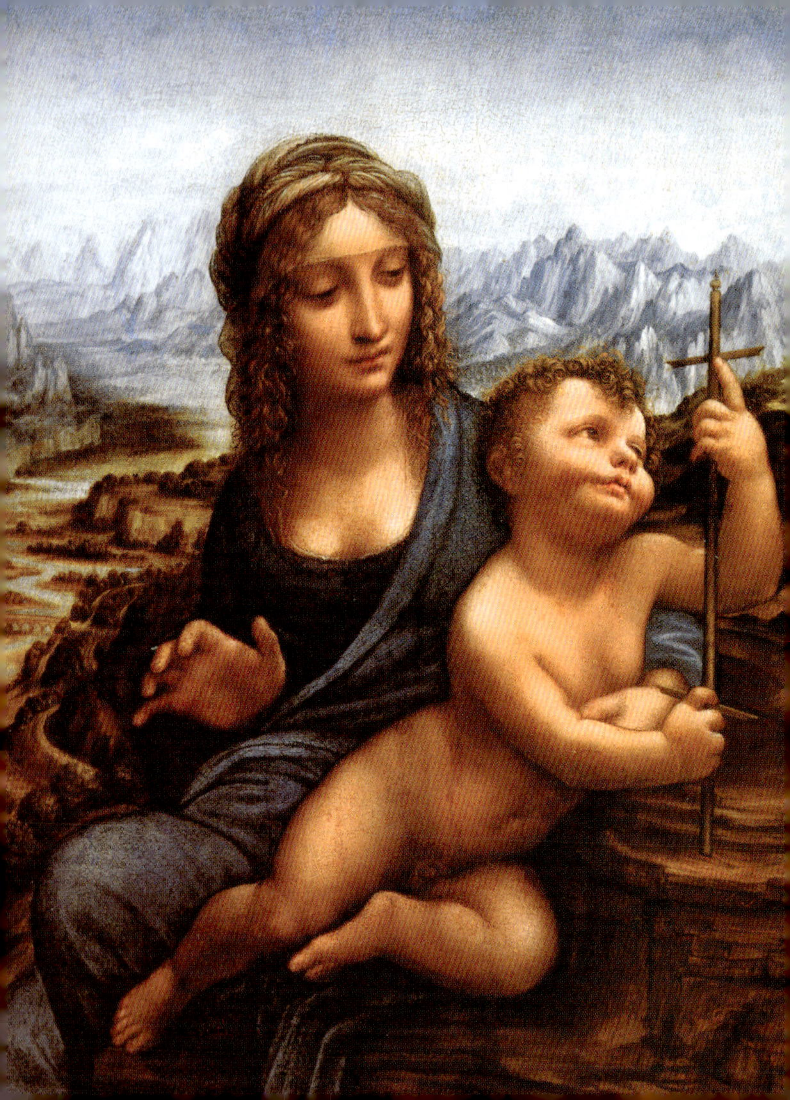

him at Mantua. We spoke freely, and arrived at this conclusion – that if he could free himself from his obligations to His Majesty the King of France without incurring disfavour, as he hoped to do within a month at the most, he would sooner serve Your Ladyship than anyone else in the world. In any event, once he has completed a little picture he is doing for a certain Robertet, a favourite of the King of France, he will immediately undertake the portrait, and send it to Your Excellency. I gave him two tokens to encourage him [*dui boni sollicitadori*]. The little picture he is working on is a Madonna who is seated as if she intended to spin yarn, and the Child has placed his foot in the basket of yarns, and has grasped the yarnwinder, and stares attentively at the four spokes, which are in the form of a cross, and as if he were longing for this cross he smiles and grips it tightly, not wishing to yield it to his mother, who appears to want to take it away from

1. This composition seems to have been first developed around 1499. Many versions exist, the most important of which are the 'Buccleuch Madonna', on loan to the National Galleries of Scotland, Edinburgh; and the 'Lansdowne Madonna' in a private collection, United States, ill. opposite

Opposite: Leonardo and assistant, Madonna of the Yarnwinder ('Lansdowne Madonna') c. 1499-1501

him. This is as much as I could get from him. Yesterday I delivered my sermon. May God grant that it bears fruits as plentiful as were its auditors.

Frater Petrus de Nuvolaria
Vice-General of the Carmelite Monks
Florence, 14 April 1501

LEONARDO DA VINCI

*Letter to Giuliano de' Medici,
Duke of Nemours,
brother of Pope Leo X,
in which Leonardo complains
about his assistant Giorgio*

1515

I was so greatly rejoiced, most Illustrious Lord, by the desired restoration of your health that it almost had the effect that my own health recovered. . . But I am extremely vexed that I have not been able completely to satisfy the wishes of your Excellency, by reason of the wickedness of that deceiver, for whom I left nothing undone which could be done for him by me and by which I might be of use to him; and in the first place his allowances were paid to him before the time, which I believe he would willingly deny, if I had not the writing signed by myself and the interpreter. And I, seeing that he did not work for me unless he had no work to do for others, which he was very careful in soliciting, invited him to eat with me, and to work afterwards near me, because, besides saving of expense, he would acquire the Italian language. (He always promised, but would never do so.) And this I did also, because that young German who makes the mirrors, was there always in the workshop, and wanted to see and to know all that was being done there and made it known outside blaming what he did not understand and because he dined with those of the Pope's guard, and then they

Opposite: A cloudburst of material possessions, c.1506-12. Inscribed 'O human misery, how many things you must serve for money'

went out with guns killing birds among the ruins; and this went on from after dinner till the evening; and when I sent Lorenzo to urge him to work he said that he would not have so many masters over him, and that his work was for Your Excellency's Wardrobe; and thus two months passed and so it went on; and one day finding Gian Niccolo of the Wardrobe and asking whether the German had finished the work for your Magnificence, he told me this was not true, but only that he had given him two guns to clean. Afterwards, when I urged him further, he left the workshop and began to work in his room, and lost much time in making another pair of pincers and files and other tools with screws; and there he worked at reels for twisting silk which he hid when any one of my people went in, and with a thousand oaths and mutterings, so that none of them would go there any more.

ANTONIO DE BEATIS

The visit of Cardinal Luigi d'Aragona to Leonardo, 10 October 1517

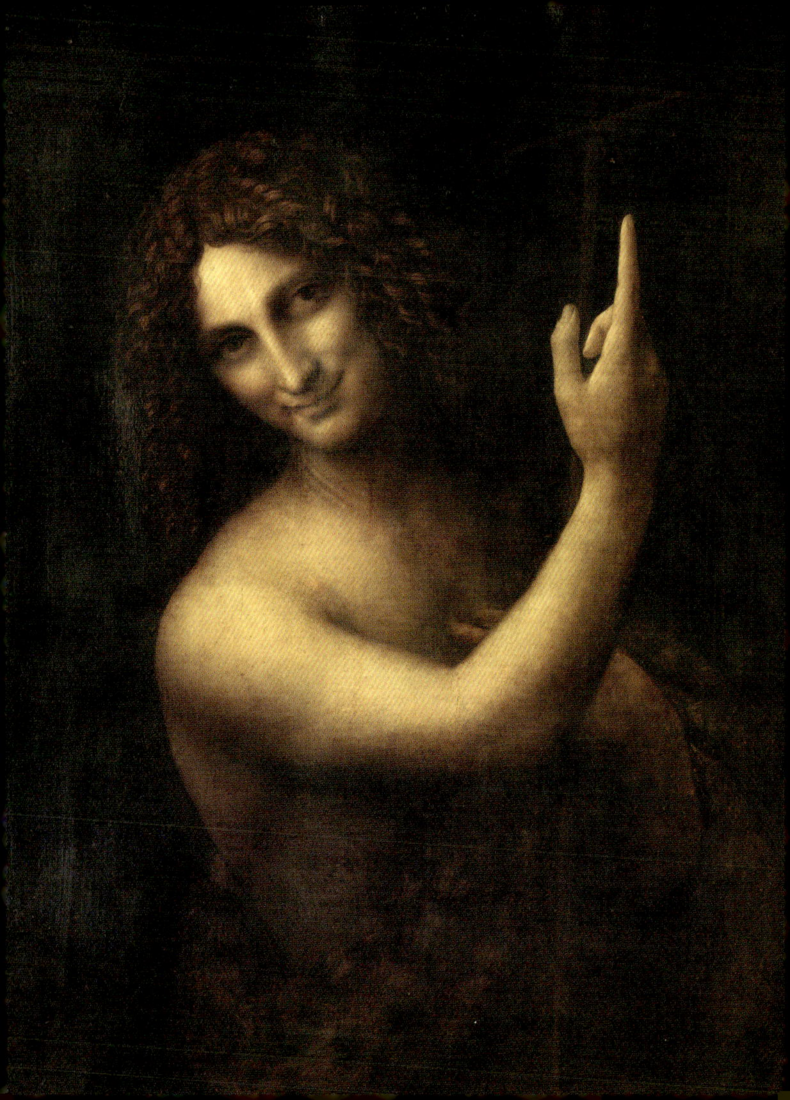

Monsignor and the rest of us went to see, in one of the outlying parts of Amboise, Messer Leonardo Vinci the Florentine, an old man of more than seventy years, the most outstanding painter of our time, who showed to his Eminence the Cardinal three pictures: one of a certain Florentine lady, painted from life, at the instance of the late Magnifico Giuliano de' Medici;[1] the other of the youthful St John the Baptist;[2] and the third of the Madonna and the Child in the lap of St Anne, the most perfect of them all.[3] One cannot indeed expect any more good work from him, as a certain paralysis has crippled his right hand. But he has a pupil, a Milanese, who works extremely well: and although Messer Leonardo can no longer paint with the sweetness which was peculiar to him, he can still draw and teach. This gentleman has written a treatise on anatomy, showing by illustrations the members, muscles, nerves, veins, joints, intestines, and whatever

1. Untraced, but possibly the Mona Lisa, Louvre, Paris, ill. p. 78
2. Louvre, Paris, ill. opposite 3. Louvre, Paris, ill. p. 119

Opposite: St John the Baptist, c. 1513-16

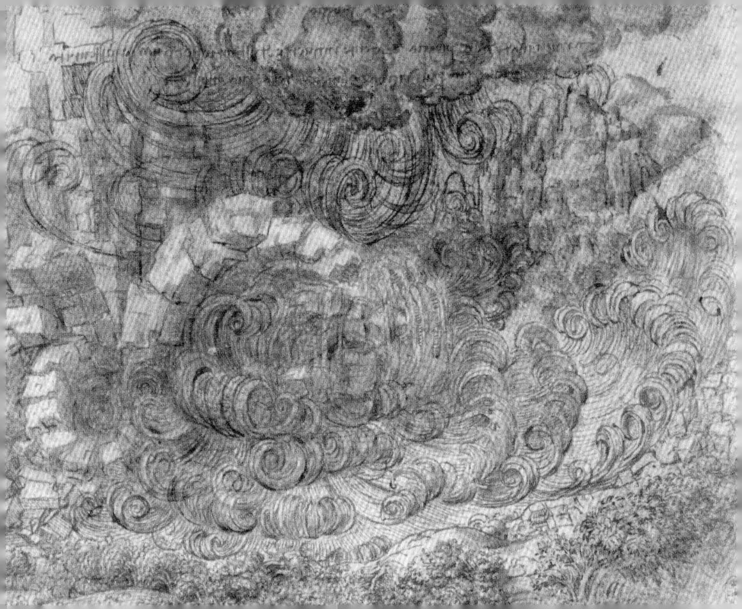

else is to discuss in the bodies of men and women, in a way that has never yet been done by anyone else. All this we have seen with our own eyes; and indeed he informed us that he had dissected more than thirty bodies, both of men and women of all ages. He has also written (or so he said) of the nature of water, and of various machines, and of other matters, which he has set down in an endless number of volumes, all in the common tongue, which, if they be published, will be profitable and delightful.

MILAN, 20 DECEMBER 1517

At the Dominican convent of Santa Maria delle Grazie, which was built by Signor Lodovico Sforza and is extremely beautiful and well cared for, we saw in the friars' refectory a Last Supper painted on the wall by Messer Leonardo da Vinci, whom we had met at Amboise.[1] This is most excellent, though it is starting to deteriorate: whether because of the dampness of the wall or because of some other oversight, I do not know. The figures in the painting are portraits,

1. Still in situ, Milan, Santa Maria delle Grazie, ill. in fold-out pp. 58-60

from life and life-size, of various court personalities and Milanese citizens of the time. At the same church we also saw a sacristy extremely rich in brocade vestments, which were likewise ordered by the late lamented Signor Lodovico.

FRANCESCO MELZI

Letter to the brothers of Leonardo about the death of the master

1 June 1519

LEONARDO
VINCI

To Ser Giuliano and his honoured brothers –

I believe that the death of your brother, Maestro Leonardo, has already been certified to you. He was to me the best of fathers, and it is impossible for me to express the grief that his death has caused me. Until the day when my body is laid under ground, I shall experience perpetual sorrow, and not without reason, for he daily showed me the most devoted and warmest affection.

His loss is a grief to everyone, for it is not in the power of nature to reproduce another such man. May the Almighty accord him everlasting rest. He passed from the present life on the 2nd of May with all the sacraments of holy Mother Church, and well disposed to receive them. The reason that he was able to make a will, leaving his goods to whom he liked, was on account of his possessing a letter from the king, exempting him *quod heredes supplicantis sint regnicolae.* Without such a letter he would not have been able to will away anything he possessed here, this being the custom of the country. Maestro Leonardo accordingly made his will, which I should have sent you sooner had I been

Opposite: Probably Francesco Melzi, Portrait of Leonardo, c. 1515–18

able to confide it to a trustworthy person. I expect that one of my uncles who has been to see me will soon return to Milan. I will dispose it in his hands, and he will faithfully remit it to you. Up to the present time I have not found other means of sending it. In so much as concerns your part in the will, Maestro Leonardo possessed in the [hospital of] Santa Maria Nuova, in the hands of the treasurer, four hundred gold crowns (*scudi di sole*) in notes which have been placed out at five per cent for the last six years counting from last October. He had also an estate at Fiesole that he wished to be distributed equally among you. There is nothing more concerning you in the will, and I will say no more except to offer you my most willing service. You will find me ready and anxious to do your will.

I recommend myself continually to you.

Given at Amboise, the 1st of June, 1519.

Please reply by the Gondi,

Tanquam fratri vestro,

Franciscus Meltius

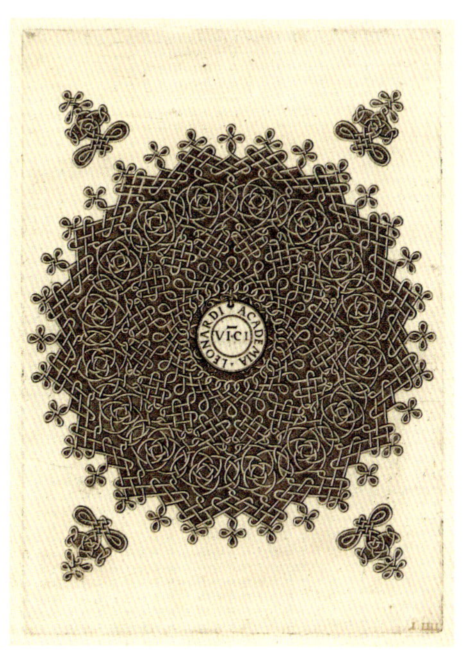

The Third Knot, engraving after Leonardo's design,
1490-1500

List of illustrations

p. 49: Madonna of the Carnation, c. 1478-80, oil on poplar panel, 62 x 48 cm, Alte Pinakothek, Munich

p. 52: Caricature of a man with bushy hair, c. 1495, pen and brown ink, 6.6 x 5.9 cm, J. Paul Getty Museum, Los Angeles

pp. 54-55: The Adoration of the Magi, 1480-81, lead white over lamp black and resin on gesso ground on poplar panel, 246 x 243 cm, Uffizi, Florence

p. 57: Half-length figure of an apostle, 1493-95, pen and brown ink over silverpoint on blue prepared paper, 14.5 x 11.3 cm, Albertina, Vienna

Fold-out, pp. 58-60: The Last Supper, 1495-98, oil and tempera on gesso, 460 x 880 cm, Santa Maria delle Grazie, Milan

p. 61: Head of Judas, 1493-95, red chalk on red prepared surface, 18 x 15 cm, Royal Collection, Windsor

p. 67: Study for an equestrian monument, c. 1485-90, metalpoint on blue prepared paper, 18.8 x 15.2 cm, Royal Collection, Windsor

pp. 70-71: Two-sided sheet of anatomical studies: The superficial anatomy of the shoulder and neck (recto); The muscles of the shoulder (verso), c. 1510-11, pen and ink with wash, over black chalk 29.2 x 19.8 cm, Royal Collection, Windsor

p. 73: Head of a youth, c. 1510-11, red and black chalks on orange-red prepared paper, 21.7 x 15.3 cm, Royal Collection, Windsor

p. 74: The Virgin and Child with St Anne and the infant St John the Baptist (Burlington House Cartoon), c. 1499-1500, charcoal (and wash?) heightened with white chalk on paper, mounted on canvas, 141.5 x 104.6 cm, National Gallery, London

pp. 77 (detail) and 78: Mona Lisa, c. 1503-17, oil on poplar panel, 77 x 53 cm, Musée du Louvre, Paris

p. 81: Unknown artist, Drawing after the Battle of Anghiari, 16th century, black chalk and gray wash, with touches of pen and brown ink, 43.5 x 56.5 cm, private collection

p. 82: Study of two warriors' heads for the Battle of Anghiari, c. 1504-5, black and red chalk, 19.2 x 18.8 cm, Szépművészeti Múzeum, Budapest

pp. 84-85: Study of fury in horses, lion and man; Rearing horse, c. 1503-4, pen and ink, wash, red chalk, 19.6 x 30.8 cm, Royal Collection, Windsor

p. 86: Study of warrior's head for the Battle of Anghiari, c. 1504-5, red chalk, 22.7 x 18.6 cm, Szépművészeti Múzeum, Budapest

p. 89: Two heads of grotesque animals, 1490-95, black chalk, pen and ink, 13.8 x 17.4 cm, Royal Collection, Windsor

pp. 91-92: Two-sided sheet of botanical studies: A branched bur-reed (recto); A bullrush (verso), red chalk on orange-red prepared paper, c. 1506-12 20.1 x 14.3 cm, Royal Collection, Windsor

p. 95: Giovan Francesco Rustici with advice from Leonardo, Preaching of St John the Baptist (with a Pharisee, left, and a Levite, right), 1506-11, bronze, 265 cm (including base), Baptistery, Florence

p. 96: Virgin and Child ('Madonna Benois'), c. 1478, oil on canvas, transferred from panel, 49 x 33 cm, State Hermitage Museum, Saint Petersburg

p. 98: Virgin and Child ('Madonna Litta'), c. 1490, 42 x 33 cm, State Hermitage Museum, Saint Petersburg

p. 102: Portrait of a Musician, c. 1485, oil on walnut panel, 44 x 32 cm, Pinacoteca Ambrosiano, Milan

p. 105: Portrait of a Woman ('La Belle Ferronière'), c. 1493-94, oil on walnut panel, 63 x 45 cm, Musée du Louvre, Paris

p. 107: Portrait of Ginevra de' Benci, c. 1474-78, oil on poplar panel, 38 x 37 cm, National Gallery of Art, Washington, DC

p. 108: Study for the head of Leda, c. 1504-6, pen and ink over black chalk, 17.7 x 14.7 cm, Royal Collection, Windsor

p. 111: The Madonna of the Rocks, c. 1495-1508, oil on poplar panel, 189 x 120 cm, National Gallery, London

p. 112: Masquerader as a lansquenet, c. 1517-18, black chalk, pen and ink, wash, on rough paper, 27.3 x 18.3 cm, Royal Collection, Windsor

p. 116: The fœtus in the womb, c. 1511, red chalk and traces of black chalk, pen and ink, with wash, 30.4 x 22 cm, Royal Collection, Windsor

p. 119: Virgin and Child with St Anne, c. 1503-19, oil on poplar panel, 168 x 112 cm, Musée du Louvre, Paris

p. 122: Detail from the Last Supper, 1495-98, oil and tempera on gesso, 460 x 880 cm, Santa Maria delle Grazie, Milan

p. 126: St Jerome, c. 1480, oil on walnut panel, 103 x 75 cm, Musei Vaticani, Rome

p. 128: Bust of a warrior in armour, 1475-80, silverpoint on cream prepared paper, 28.7 x 21.1 cm, British Museum, London

p. 130: Design for a portable bridge, c. 1485, pen, ink and wash, 14.8 x 22.1 cm, Codex Atlanticus f. 71v, Veneranda Biblioteca Ambrosiana, Milan